Finding PEACE
Discovering JOY

A Guide to Living Happily Every Day

Y. B. Gray

May peace, joy and happiness be yours always!!

This book is dedicated to all the people in the world who want peace and joy in their lives so that others may know it as well.

To my wonderful husband Chris, my six inspirational children, my parents and all my family for their continued love and support throughout the years.

To my dear friends Jean, Kim S., and Kim B., who continue to be some of my biggest fans and cheerleaders with every endeavor.

To artisan Dennis G., my clients, and all the people I have been fortunate to know throughout the years, for sharing your experiences, wisdom, and advice.

Contents

Author's Note

No matter one's age or profession, the ability to find peace and in so doing discovering joy can create a fuller, happier, and more productive life. This book was written as a response to the inquiries of clients, friends, and family: "How can I be happy every day?" The idea of being "happy" every day is not to say that bad stuff does not come up. There are times that you may not be able to have a smile on your face. A person can generally be happy even though daily life presents new and sometimes very complicated situations. Bad things do happen. How they are handled is as important as your perceptions of what happened.

Finding peace in one's life and realizing the joy and general happiness on a day-to-day basis provide a means to handle times of stress with more grace and to develop methods of coping with the difficult times. It also provides a way to step back from situations and make better decisions based on the facts involved, instead of reacting from a purely emotional and fear based level.

Have you ever met a person who seemed so calm or happy that his or her very presence calmed you down or made you happy? How would you like to be that person? Often those people seem to have a ton of friends or at least no obvious enemies. Why is that?

There isn't a magic pill or one word answer to find peace and discover joy. This book can't answer every question or give examples to every possible scenario life can throw you. After reading this book, you will have a larger body of knowledge to help you respond to different situations. Just taking a moment to calm one's mind or at least put the situation into a little better perspective can make all the difference. If stress can be reduced and opportunities for peace and joy found, then life is better for the knowledge.

Go in peace and may you find peace, joy and happiness daily.

YBG

Introduction

A story

There was once a person searching for that "something" that could not be attained by wealth and material possessions. He owned multiple houses and cars and the newest technologies money could buy. Cash at hand was never a problem. He had degrees from the top universities and belonged to exclusive organizations. He would speak with the greatest academic minds, for he was fortunate to have a career that afforded him the audience of great scientific and literary people. His popularity and wealth got him into the well known clubs and hangouts that were reserved for the elite. But with all his wealth, popularity and education, something eluded him. There was this *thing* missing that he could not name or fully conceptualize. Restlessness took over his mind, and calm was not within his grasp. This yearning for something that he could not identify caused him much distress and agitation.

One day he was waiting in line at the local café for his coffee with an expression on his face as if he were deep in thought and not happy. Upon seeing him, an older lady noticed his demeanor and could tell that he was troubled. She asked the man what was wrong. He told her that he had attained wealth, popularity, and an impressive education. Yet, for some reason, he was restless and still wanting for *something*. He had everything he could want and was generally enjoying his life, except for this *thing* that he was missing. She nodded her head as if she could relate. She looked at him for a moment and started to share her story.

I too had everything, a family, a successful career, national awards, and notoriety while still having privacy. I had everything I could want and retired with prestige, a great pension, and friends. Yet I knew I was missing something. One day I woke up to find myself comfortably retired, with quiet when I wanted and places to go if I wanted to do something. I volunteered and felt I was needed and appreciated. But I could not stand being without this *something* I could not name. I knew it was more than mere restlessness but could not put my finger on it. Later that day, I went to a coffee shop. I probably looked a little like you do now. I was agitated and not knowing what I was yearning for or what was bugging me. Then I lost my temper at how long the people were taking to fill the orders. In the middle of my anger one of the patrons told me, "Peace out, lady." After realizing my rudeness I calmed down. I apologized, got my beverage, and thought of what the young man had said. "Peace out." It dawned on me that I did not know what in the world it meant to "have" peace. I searched for the definition and asked my friends. I did all kind of stuff and finally figured it out.

The café attendant took her order and then knowing she needed to go, she turned to the man and quickly said, "Find peace and everything will work itself out."

He wanted to tell the woman to wait, and he wanted her to tell him what she knew. If this was his way to stop the agitation, then he wanted to know what she found out. After he made his order, he quickly went to pick up his drink but she was gone. Later that day, after running a couple errands, he went home with an unsettling thought in regards to his conversation with the woman at the coffee shop. Did he have to wait until retirement to attain this ability to no longer be restless, to gain this *thing* that he was missing? Was it as simple as finding peace? If so, what does that mean, "Find peace"? He went to the dictionary and looked up the definition only to be disappointed that there wasn't a road map or directions to "finding" this peace. The definitions only mentioned silence or an inner form of peace or contentment. What in the world did that mean? So he went to the Internet search engines and came up with everything from not being in war to some meditative mumbo-jumbo. What is this "peace" that the lady was referring to? He continued his normal day-to-day activities and thought of this missing *thing* called "peace" in the back of his mind, amidst his full and active life.

One day, while waiting for his friends for a night out on the town, he decided to kill time at a nearby park. He parked on the dirt parking lot and made his way past the playground lined with strollers and talking women and decided to continue to the nearby lake. While sitting on a park bench looking out onto a small man-made lake lined with trees, he started to reflect on this *thing* called peace.

As he was thinking, a serene aged woman who had been feeding the ducks came and sat on an adjoining bench. She looked to the man and observed that he seemed pensive. He looked troubled, for his face was tight, lips pursed, not so much in anger but with a bewildered look. She ventured to say "hello."

He was startled that she was there and felt awkward by the surprise. He returned the greeting with an obligatory "hello." She continued to ramble on, now that she seemed to have gotten his attention.

"What a great day, the sun is shining and the sky just has a few wispy clouds. The flowers are all in bloom, and the sweet fragrance is so subtle and pleasant. The grass is green, and after yesterday's rain the air smells so clean and fresh. Hardly anyone is working, and everyone around looks happy. It's one of those days where you can lose yourself in the silence of this calm place. If you can relax enough, you might find peace in a busy life."

She spoke so quickly that it seemed she had not taken a breath between any of her words. He felt the urge to figure out who this person was, so he turned to look at her with more intent to know who was addressing him. The man looked to the aged woman. Though her face was lined with wrinkles, she was probably very beautiful in youth. The lines around her mouth were as if she had done nothing but smiled for years. Thinking she was a bit strange to ramble on with a stranger but figuring her ramblings might have some answers, he asked her what she thought peace was. Her reply was, "Peace is the ability to be calm and know everything is going to be okay. You can sit and the world would still turn and your life won't be messed up because of it."

He looked down for a moment to ponder her words and when he came out of his thoughts, he looked up to see she had gone.

After tossing and turning all night with the lady's answer replaying in his head, he decided to take a day off. He cancelled his plans for another day on the green with the guys from the office. There was no way he could focus on anything with the way he felt. Instead, he figured that he should take a break, just one day: no work, no phone, no television or radio. He remembered overhearing a conversation at work of this nice spa that had a great view of the mountains. The person had said it really help him to "chill out" after having a tough week. He called to make sure he could get a spot for that day and set off to what he hoped would be a place he could clear his mind.

His hour-long drive was without traffic and wound its way up the mountains. As he approached the resort, he saw that the spa location was made to look like an oversize but luxurious log cabin. It sat atop a hill miles from a dormant ski lodge waiting for activity with the upcoming ski season. He checked in and decided to enjoy the services the spa had to offer. After getting a soothing facial and rejuvenating massage, he took a relaxing dip in the pool. Later he casually got dressed and leisurely ate a five-course dinner served with wine and a decadent dessert. Sitting out in the beautifully tended floral gardens which were void of people, he watched the few puffy clouds blow by.

The sunset behind the mountains cascaded the land with soft red, violet and orange hues of light. The effect of the light in the gardens gave the landscape a feel of a deep and quiet calm. At dusk it felt as if nature decided to rest itself after providing him that brilliance of color, light, and overall splendor. It was as if nature too wanted to share with him this time of calm. This man who was in search of peace found he yearned never to leave this quiet and calm place. The calm of the day brought him an inner happiness he had not known. It was at that moment he realized that he had found "peace," and in doing so discovered a joy he could not explain. He then remembered the words of the lady from the park: "Peace is the ability to be calm and know everything is going to be okay. You can sit and the world would still turn and your life won't be messed up because of it." At this thought he drifted into sleep.

Like the man in the story, many of us are looking for that peace, that joy. Some find it at a resort or spa after becoming fully relaxed from the services that are provided. The person is able to relax and look around with a newfound appreciation for the beauty that surrounds him or her. We can't all go to a spa, and those who can should not spend their whole life trying to escape the world and find peace in this way. This man had everything money could buy. He had friends and prestige but had not taken the time in his active life to think of anything more. When he achieved all he could imagine, the one thing he couldn't imagine was the peace that money and fame could not buy. But given the idea to search for it, his resources made it easier for him to create an opportunity and with his lack of worry he was able to figure it out.

Chapter 1
What Is Peace and Joy?

As for the man in the story at the beginning of this book who knew "something" was missing, peace is often elusive. By the end of the story he did find a level of peace, but can we say that peace will last? Is it a peace that is truly calm or just exhaustion? The peace that he felt was more a sense of the moment or short-term peace, versus a sense of wellbeing. How can we make this sense of calm not short term but a part of everyday life? Most people have an idea of what peace and joy is, but find it difficult to experience such calm happiness daily. In today's world and modern work environment, we often find it difficult to remember who we are and where we are supposed to be at any given time. Therefore, keeping up with the needs, wants, and pulls of our everyday lives is very demanding. This term "finding peace" is an active term. It means that you have to actively look for and seek peace in your life. This peace can be found in the mundane of the silence of a sitting room or the marvel of the natural beauty of a rainbow. A more personal calm can be experienced by knowing no matter what happens at home or work, in the end all will turn up right and good in the world.

In sign language the sign for "peace" incorporates two terms. It begins with the sign for "transform" and ends in "silence." That transformation is an active one that requires engagement of the individual and not expecting happenstance to create that silence for you. The moment that this "peace" is achieved is generally followed with the feeling of joy. Oftentimes joy and happiness are used synonymously. Yet, others would beg to differ. Some see happiness as the equivalent to getting that close parking space at the mall. Yet for others, joy would be in the recognition of being an "employee of the month" and earning a close parking space. One person might find joy in climbing a mountain while another finds it when they finish reading a good book. As all things that are related to the idea of a "feeling," there is no clear or simple explanation. The definition is broad because those who do experience "peace and joy" often value and experience the feeling differently. While peace and joy are experienced differently, the result is generally the sense of positive wellbeing.

To say that everyone is going to experience peace and joy the same way would be a mistake. The idea and experience of peace is in large part based on our prior experiences and our expectations about the level of calm and happiness we expect. What we think peace should be like and how we think our reaction to any given situation should be to a large part is in how we experience peace and our overall level of joy.

Joy is also defined based on the ideas and conceptions of what it means to be happy. We extrapolate the idea of joy from the various levels of happiness that we experience, from simple pleasures to euphoria. For people who have had a hard life, where the bare necessities such as food and shelter are sparse and living conditions are difficult, happiness is found in the experience of receiving three meals or even one full meal in a day. That "happiness" will increase when they know they can earn their meals and experience full stomachs again. The heightened happiness, "joy," is experienced in seeing the family happy, full, and secure. Happiness is in the experience, and "joy" is in the sharing of the experience.

Taking time to consider the idea of peace and joy helps to create a "reset" if you will, of our lives. We can get so hung up in the details of having to pay bills, working a job, taking care of other family members, or trying to survive life as we know it. If we do not take the time to see the peace and joy that is in our lives and/or create a means for experiencing that peace and joy, then will we be able to understand where we belong in our world or where in our lives the idea of peace and joy exist? This level of awareness is a vital part of life towards understanding what makes us happy. Knowing what makes us upset or mad tends to be easier and are often subjects we dwell upon for longer periods of time.

Some people think that dwelling a moment on the idea of what makes a person happy is selfish, conceited, or narcissistic. Instead let's consider that those who seem selfish, conceited, or narcissistic do not know what truly makes them happy. They dwell on themselves until they find something that will make them happy, only to miss the idea of peace and joy altogether. If we fit in this category, does the previous statement sound true? We go from thing to thing, person to person, and still are not able to escape the world of ourselves. To learn about and only focus on ourselves can be a lonely place to be.

If we can learn what makes us happy, to have peace in our lives and experience joy on a daily basis, it is almost impossible to be selfish, conceited, or narcissistic. We have heard, "Home is where the heart is." Imagine if peace, joy, and overall happiness were where our heart is. What a life that would be. This is where the heart and mind work together. This is why it is worth considering what peace and joy means in our lives and conceptualizing living in peace and joy daily.

What does it feel like to find peace and discover joy?

When we think of the term "feel," are we thinking about using our five senses in order to engage in the activity, action, or feeling? In the terms mentioned of the five senses, it would feel something like the contentment of just breathing and living. What does that mean? Have you ever woken up in the morning and you felt like you really slept well? At the same time, the idea of laying down staring at the ceiling and enjoying that restful lull is enough to hold you through the day. It's the feeling that you don't owe your time to anyone else other than yourself. In the sense of feeling peace, this description is one that would be tangible to most. The physical feeling where all bodily extremities are relaxed, almost limp, the mind is awake, but no physical strain being experienced is another example of a person experiencing peace and contentment. When nothing hurts and the body is not exhausted or in want for more sleep or rest is another example. The physical peace of lying in a hammock with no need to go anywhere at any time without demands or restrictions would sometimes fall under the description of bliss or a peaceful joy.

The feeling of peace in an "inward" sense is often attributed to "non-stressed days." But more than a lack of stressors, there is a feeling of security and connectivity with the world around us. Some may use the word "Zen," or affiliate the inward feeling of peace as something that comes from the act of meditation or the clearing of the mind. Many times "peace" is something we search for or is actively worked toward. Some would say it is the emptying or the opening of the mind, but both require the sense of activity and the action of finding this kind of peace.

Some would say that internal peace is harder to achieve than the physical peace of a quiet room. Have you ever been in a quiet room, maybe a waiting room, and you wish for the television to be on or to at least read a book or look at pictures in a magazine? People placed in an empty room would prefer not be alone without the want to "do" something or have some sound, noise, or something else. Sometimes people are too afraid to have silence, for their thoughts might lead them to think about those things they do not want to think about or to confront. Sometimes meeting the silence of space is the noise that fills our minds. Some people are too scared to deal with the deep thoughts that confront who they are in real life. Ultimately they find themselves having to reflect on what their life looks like and then how they are portrayed by other people. They resist seeing if their genuine selves, the person they really are, matches the person that they project themselves to be. The feelings around such thoughts hinder an inner peace from flourishing in an individual. This also means that these issues need to be confronted. Accepting oneself is all part of the process of finding peace and discovering joy in one's personal life.

Finding peace and discovering joy as a process

The artisan

A wood carver and artisan works with his hands in the creation of usable wooden items, working with the shape, grain, and natural color of wood that would otherwise be discarded or left to rot. He experiences moments of peace and joy throughout the creation of his pieces of wood art. His creations vary from coat racks and quilt racks to benches, lamps, and more. He experiences moments of joy and a feeling of calm and accomplishment wrapped up in the feeling of peace and joy, along with those "aha" moments—those instances where imagination and creativity can turn into a conceptualized reality.

The experience of having the wood reveal what it would become is a multi-step process. The "aha" moment of "knowing" what the wood will be is a momentary source of peace and joy. Moving forward in the process of taking off the bark and "discovering" the true grain becomes another source of joy. Looking at the wood itself to reaffirm by its shape and grain that the creation intended for this piece of wood fits the initial idea, inception, and creation helps to feel even more creative pleasure during this process. If problems or mistakes happen along the way, it is but a setback. The wood can still be smoothed out, and with a little imagination and flexibility in design it will still arrive into its finished product. When the cutting and carving is done, seeing its singular form becomes another source of peace and joy. Putting the pieces together, smoothing the texture, and realizing the finished product is closer at hand presents another moment of enjoyment.

In anticipation for the project's completion, excitement creeps in, an impetus to finishing this product. When the labor of creating, shaping, assembling, and finishing work is done and the finished usable piece of art is completed, the knowledge of its creation and the experience of its evolution and finally its existence creates the euphoria of accomplishment. For the woodworking artist knows all is well with this creation and the joy of knowing that the wood has become what it is meant to be is a peace and joy that he holds. These simple moments can lead to those lasting memories that lend itself to be a catalyst for greater peace and longer lasting joy.

Finding peace and discovering joy in terms of a process is most relevant in times of hardship and difficulty. This artisan story is only one example of recognizing peace and joy in one's work. This book will examine and explain other ways of experiencing peace and joy as a process in life and a way to troubleshoot times of difficulty.

If we encounter peace and joy, wouldn't it be better that we never know the difference?

Maybe this is the ultimate question in regard to finding peace and discovering joy. If we never experienced it, then we can't be sad or feel any sense of loss when peace and joy is harder to experience or seemingly non-existent. But when we are in the state of true peace, a real sense of joy, and the extreme pleasurable calm of the moment, hours or day can make up for so much prior discontent, sadness, difficulty, and pain. A good example of this is at the birth of a child. The mother may have had morning sickness, back pain, bed rest, and twenty-four hours of labor, all for the climax of the birth of her child. Once that baby is in her arms, tears of joy and a profound sense that something great has happened tends to exude from the joy of the mother, the pride of the father, and the celebration of new life within the family to friends and the neighboring community. The encounter of peace and joy makes life evermore worth living and something never worth relinquishing.

What are the strengths in having a peaceful and joyous life?

There is solace in living a peaceful and joyful life. Some people would say they feel blessed and cheerful most of the time. To have this kind of life is more of a lifestyle, a way to appreciate more about what life is truly about. Life is not just going through the motions every day of getting up, going to work or school, eating, and sleeping. Yes, this is what we do, but not all of what we do. How do we take care of ourselves? The people around us, who are they to us?

When you can be peaceful and generally happy, you will come to recognize that you are incredibly special and unique. Peaceful or not, you are important. There is a reason you're here, and it is not to torture colleagues and bully peers. Someone once said that a person has to fight their way to the top. Why? What is the top? The strength about living happily is the fact that you no longer measure success by material things.

Yes, we all need shelter, food, clothing, and a reason to work so hard. When speaking of material things, we are talking about five cars when there are only two drivers or the three rooms in our homes full of clothes. When a person is generally happy, too much of anything starts to seem excessive. A person can be a millionaire, have the mansion, the car, and a furnished home, be happy, and yet not have too much. It is only when that person no longer knows who they are and falls into the trap of the society around them that says "things are the measure of success" that peace can become difficult to attain. Anyone can be happy. Being in peace and filled with joy is not only for religious or spiritual gurus.

There is freedom in being at peace and filled with joy. Appreciating what you have is a strength that peace and joy provide. It is good to have goals for what you would like and work toward. That dream of owning a particular car or house is perfectly fine. Appreciating what you have on your way to better and bigger things is also good. The freedom found in peace and joy is the freedom to know that no matter what happens you will go through it and come out the other side. When life is at its hardest you will find ways to help yourself while helping others. When bad people come across your path and peace and joy seems further away, you will know others who can help you find calm again. Living in peace and joy also serves as a reminder that you are not alone and that you are important.

Chapter 2
Obstacles to
Peace and Joy

Wherever there is peace, joy, and everyday happiness, there are always those people or things that threaten or weaken our progress towards living a peaceful and joyous life. If you can think of something that reminds you of happiness, joy, calm, and security, it doesn't take much to think of the direct opposite. It is feelings of despair, depression, negative thoughts, cup half-empty thinking, and negative baggage that we carry with us from our childhood that gets in the way of peace and joy. The past in general, with our feelings of wellbeing or the lack thereof, fear, guilt, or just the disbelief that we deserve happiness are obstacles to peace and joy daily.

First, let us get one thing clear. You deserve to be happy. The very fact that you live, breathe, feel, and love gives you the right to be happy, to know peace and experience joy every day. Life is yours to live! Life is not without troubles, but to survive in times of troubles and to thrive in times of plenty is to be celebrated. You have the right to be sad at times and cry when you need to, but remember that you will be happy again with time. Once we have agreed that we will allow ourselves to have peace and joy, we can discuss the other threats to our own happiness.

Physicality

Much of our day is predicated on our physical wellbeing, which often sets our mood. If we wake up in pain, our day is different than if we wake feeling fully rested, relaxed, and rejuvenated.

If a person has chronic illnesses and wakes up in pain every day, it is understandable that they are sad, upset, or short-tempered. But does a person have to choose to stay in this mood? Sometimes the pain is so difficult that getting out of bed is a chore. But if that person gets out of bed, pushes themselves out of the house to experience just one more day of living and maybe making a difference in just one other person's life that day, then the pain is lessened ever so slightly because that person has made the world a better place. We are not talking an earth-shattering difference, but one that says, "Because I exist the world has become better." Believe it or not, it is possible to smile beyond hurt and discomfort. You may have to start with a grimace or a smirk. You might have to work at it, but if you make the effort and keep at it, you will be able to do it. We have seen time and again how sharing a smile can help the people around us. Sometimes, knowing that we can do a little more than "nothing at all" is enough to make it a good day.

When we sleep, we need to get enough of it for our bodies to do well the following day. In Western culture, we think of morning as the start of a new day. In some cultures, the evening and sleep itself is the start of the new day, and waking up in the morning is the continuation. What a beautiful thought, to start the day off right by going to sleep. Sleep allows the body to relax, heal, the mind to rest and let the subconscious work on the troubles of the prior day. Even someone who has no physical ailments will feel tired and not at their best without enough restful sleep.

Get moving. If you know you are out of shape, what are you doing to improve the situation? You don't need a gym. Just go walking for ten minutes. These walks can start out as leisurely, and then you can see how far you can go in five minutes and return. See what you are capable of. Our bodies like a little workout. The more you feel like doing nothing, the more important it is that you get out. If you live in a climate where doing outside activity is physically too dangerous, think about going to the mall and taking a few laps around. If you are homebound because of weather or transportation, march in place or dance to your favorite music in an open area of your house. You don't even have to dance well, just move to your favorite music, whether it is orchestral, country, rock, rhythm and blues or the various other choices we have. Try to listen to positive music versus the morbid or depressing soundtracks. What we hear can affect our mood and should be considered. Just getting your body active helps to also clear your head and work toward a better mood.

Eat and drink to fill the needs of your body. We all need to eat. What we eat does count. Flavorful foods can still be our choice, just let it also be something with nutritional value. A little junk food here and there may seem like a treat, but don't make it a habit. If after you eat you have digestive issues or you feel a bit ill, check into the fact that you may be allergic to something you ate or need medical advice on not having such a bad reaction to your meal. Sometimes we get irritable if our digestive track is bothering us. Avoiding those things that cause physical distress may be a good thing to add in your goals.

Sleep Deprived

A person does not have to be a doctor to know that when you don't get enough sleep it is harder to think well. People on too little sleep tend to get more agitated, even clumsy and disorderly. If the sleep deprivation is bad enough, a person can be very dangerous driving or handling heavy equipment. Many people who have constantly gone without enough sleep may find themselves falling asleep at the wheel or swerving off the road. Alcohol does not have to be involved in a case of a sleep deprived driver for that person to end up killing themselves or another person.

Have you ever stayed up and out too late on a Sunday and were expected to be at work early the next day? Many people do. It doesn't matter how old a person may be or whether the person is a male or female, sleep is an important factor in how alert we are and the way we experience our day.

Have you ever had a coworker who stayed up too late the night before and showed up to work the next day? Let's say, he set his alarm Sunday night because he stayed out and did not want to be late to work the next day. When the alarm clock sounded, the snooze button was immediately pressed and he enjoyed fifteen minutes of extended sleep. The alarm goes off again and he wakes up looking at the clock wondering why it went off so late. He gets up and makes his way to the bathroom, showers, gets dressed, crams some food down his throat, and hopes the coffee at work is decent. Maybe he chooses to wait at a drive through for a caffeine fix. He gets to work just in time. It is Monday and there is a meeting in thirty minutes. He has a briefing to give and has five minutes to review the material. He hurriedly goes to the meeting and reports on the project. In the middle of speaking his stomach growls, but he continues his report hoping nobody noticed. After the meeting he leaves to go back to his cubicle to only to notice that he was wearing blue socks with brown shoes, while wearing black pants and a grey sweater. His pants zipper was down and the piece of paper he handed out was the draft of the report not the final copy he was planning to hand out.

If this does not sound like a scenario that has happened at work, maybe something similar has happened in your experience. The setting and specifics may be different, but the feeling of being hurried, not ready, or less than comfortable with the start of the day may be an occurrence to which you can relate. Maybe manic Mondays are a result of lack of sleep, lack of a breakfast, and feeling as though you are being put on the spot unprepared.

Now let's imagine that you got enough sleep and woke up just before the buzzer of the alarm went off. You turned off the alarm before it made a sound so your day can start calmly. You shower and dress and make breakfast. You have your cup of tea or coffee just the way you like it and take a moment more to make sure you have what you need for the day before you leave for work. You go to work and say "hi" to the other colleagues who showed up for work early. Before the meeting, you decide to look over the report and notice it was the wrong printout. You get the correct report printed in time. You go to the meeting and are the first one there ready for your report. You take the time to talk to colleagues as they enter. You do the report, go to your cubicle, and continue the day.

The second scenario is not much different than the first. The biggest difference is the feeling of being rushed. Starting the day rested and fed helps to provide us the time and energy to be at our best throughout the day. We are a bit less alert without enough sleep. Not eating a good breakfast adds to the physical stress we put on our bodies. Providing our bodies the nutrients and rest we need in order to be at our best, in addition to keeping our level of stress in check through the means of relaxation or keeping a clear head, we can be more alert to the opportunities to find peace and discover joy throughout the day.

We put our bodies through a lot of stress physically when we do not eat right or sleep enough for our bodies to heal from the damages or the physiological stressors of the day. Another way to reduce stress and become more relaxed is simply getting enough sleep, drinking enough water, and eating good food. To experience peace and joy, we have to want it and work toward it. Relaxation and bringing our minds to a calm and anxiety-free state assist in the effort to allow us to become more aware of the opportunities for peace.

Mental challenges

Mental threats to peace and joy are our biggest areas of concern. These areas that hinder us come from environmental, genetic, and psychological conditioning. We deserve to be happy, and yet depression, anxiety, or the baggage of our past and the abuse from others, of substances, and our own feelings of worth can all hinder truly living a happy life.

We all have moments of questioning ourselves and our abilities, but to linger on such negative thoughts is not healthy. This is where positive influences such as friends, family, or a feel-good movie can help, along with positive sayings and words of encouragement on a poster or books that you think are funny. Books that remind you of happy times, such as photo albums or comics, are worthy of a location and spot on your bookcase. We all need to create support mechanisms that help us to gauge accurately the situation or at least not let any situation get too negative or out of hand.

We all have short periods of bad, sad, and depressing times. When these times turn into long periods or the depression becomes too all-consuming, get help. If you are having issues with past experiences that have resulted in too much fear, anxiety, or reliving the situation, please seek professional help from counselors, psychologists, or psychiatrists. Often these people are trained and have had the experience working with many people with similar concerns or difficulties. You are not alone, and seeking professional help is no longer looked at negatively in the social sphere. Take care to deal with this issue so you can move on in all areas of your life.

Our outlook on life needs to be as positive as possible. If you think to yourself, "Life stinks and then you die," you are the person who has to pay attention to this section. Sometimes things happen. Sometimes horrible things happen; we may feel horrible and negative, but we choose not to wallow in that sadness or discontent. Choose to go through it, around it, under it, or whatever, but choose not to be crushed by it. Life is what you make it. Make it as happy as you can by seeing what good there is to see. If you have a favorite gum, movie, cup, plant, whatever that favorite thing is, there is a reason for it. Usually it's because it makes you happy. Remember a time of joy, or the type of food that fills you or tastes great. Life is not bad. It is how we choose to see life that can make it conducive to overall happiness. Choose to be happy.

Most people are not without worry or apprehension. Though many people know of this idea of "peace," many do not experience the feeling of peace within themselves or their environmental and living conditions. Most people know what it means to be happy and experience a momentary joy but cannot hold onto the feeling. Circumstances, experiences, and possibly distrust of people, places, or things can often deter a person from finding peace and discovering joy on a daily basis. In order to find peace and discover joy, we need to be more aware of ourselves and those distractions that keep us from a generally happy life.

So how can we attain peace for more than mere moments or say that we are "living" in the state of peace? That's a little trickier. How would you answer the question? Do you worry? How is your state of life at this moment? Do you feel like you can sit for a moment? Could you tell yourself everything is all right and enjoy the moment? Does it feel like you are always catching up with life instead of being able to live it? Thinking in this direction and having the time to figure all this out while living our lives can be daunting and sometimes seems impossible, and yet we are always expected to have it (life) together.

That's the catch isn't it? The idea that we can put our lives, worries, responsibilities, and anxieties aside so we can experience this *thing* called "peace and joy" can seem elusive and unrealistic. Peace seems to be something we stumble upon, given the right conditions and our ability to live "in the moment"—or is it? What does it mean to live? What does it mean to live in the moment? Are there conditions to living either way, and is there a difference? It is obvious that these larger questions of life cannot be answered in a single volume of any book, let alone a collection of books. We can certainly start in a direction that will help. Focusing on these questions with the bent that we are searching for peace and hoping along the way to experience the joy that is achievable through a peaceful life is a good start. This peaceful and happier life will certainly assist in coming to grips with life in general.

It is not enough to want peace and joy and overall happiness in life. Anything worth our thoughts and time requires activity and effort. Just like money does not grow on trees, peace and joy doesn't pop up out of nowhere. Unlike money, peace and joy does not have to cost so much in time or physical work. Ever looked for a set of keys only to find that they were in front of your face or exactly where you thought you put it the whole time you were searching? The opportunities for peace and joy are always around us; it is up to us to recognize the opportunities and choose to seize the moment to experiencing them. It is in times of stress, emotional and physical distress and being tired, physically, emotionally, and mentally, that we have the most difficulty in realizing we could be happier even with the hardship.

If we can find ways to remain calm and to relax during trying times, we all might be happier and maybe a bit healthier. Trying to live a peaceful life is not to say that we need a life of silence. Instead the need would be for a life in which we can remain calm even in times of trials. When opportunities of peace, joy, or even simple happy moments present themselves, we can be aware of the moment and seize it. There are many ways to improve our ability to experience peace, and learning to relax would definitely help.

Some may say, "Oh yeah, meditate." True, meditation would help to bring people to a calm state, and therefore I would suggest that this is a very good means of emptying the mind of troublesome thoughts. This practice allows for a more relaxed and peaceful mental and physical state. In this case, meditation is a tool for working towards calm and self-awareness. There are so many forms of meditation that there are whole bookshelves in libraries and book stores dedicated to the various forms. Many religions and philosophical beliefs incorporate meditation or meditative prayer in their traditions and practices. Often breath and posture is an integral part of the meditative process. Whenever someone is experiencing a lot of stress or anxiety, someone may say aloud, "Just breathe." This concept that our breathing can control our emotional and physiological status is well known, even to those who do not practice meditation on a normal basis. In suspense thrillers, the screen may be a jumble of graphics. People are watching the screen, but during that one dramatic scene you could hear the stillness and silence of the audience holding its breath. Breath is *that* connected to our emotional and mental state.

A relaxing breathing exercise

If you don't know any meditation or breathing exercises, there are many books on the subject that explore the various ways of relaxing through controlled breathing. One of the simplest forms of breathing exercises is the practice of closing your eyes while sitting upright in your chair.

Lay your hands in your lap with your palms up. Have the back part of your wrists lying on your lap so they are supported. You can relax your shoulders and arms without your hands falling off your legs. Breathe slowly in through your nose and out through your mouth. Relax your face. If you are in a state of stress, it may seem difficult. Take turns lightly massaging your forehead in a circular clockwise position with one hand (imagine you are looking at a clock to get started then lose the image and relax). Then lightly stroke your face with your fingertips (both hands) along your upper jaw line. Start below the temples, lightly stroking the upper jaw line and ending below the nose, until the muscles feel a little more relaxed. Resume the restful sitting position and try again. You may notice your face relaxing.

The reason for the light massage at the jaw line is to also relax the muscles at the upper and lower jaw. This will assist in making sure the muscles that may have been used to clench and grind the back of your teeth know it is time to relax. If your face is relaxed, don't be surprised to hear the sound of your breath escaping through your teeth.

Imagine all the tensions and anxiety of the day leaving your body with each exhale of breath. With every inhale through your nose, imagine life-giving breath energizing every pore and cell in your body. Imagine strength to continue the day being given to you with each breath. Then open your eyes when you can feel your body responding to this exercise in a state of relaxation. Sometimes you may want to stay still in this position.

If you are at work or school, you will find yourself in a little better state of mind than you were before you attempted the exercise. While attempting this exercise, if you were thinking of the problems of the day instead of the thought portion of the exercise as stated, then try again. No thoughts would be better than stressful thoughts. This simple exercise helps you become more relaxed. Additionally this should help you clear your mind of the toxic negative talk or worry we often subject ourselves to. Meditation and breathing doesn't have a corner on the market for relaxation or reducing stress, it is just one exercise from the choice of many that most people are capable of using.

Free yourself from worry

There are many ways to free yourself from worry. There are a lot of religions, philosophies, and people of faith in general that would say, "Pray; you have to believe in a god(s) that will bring you into that state." To this, I also say, "Good for you." Most belief systems have a form of prayer to calm and focus one to a relaxed state or a focus outside the reality of the physical world that can open a person to experiencing peace. Many prayers also come with some form of meditative processes, which can include chants, repetitive prayers, and tools such as prayer beads. Though the prayer beads may have different names in the various faith traditions, the effect of directed thought with the help of this tool is the same. Giving up the worries and asking for help from a deity that one believes will grant the request frees the person in prayer to think of other things than that event or set of thoughts that cause distress.

Many people find peace when they attend services at some religious house of worship or with the development and attainment of some form of religious or philosophical decision. Churches, synagogues, temples, mosques, and other houses of worship offer a sense of community. These serve as places where a person can often share worry as well as joy and receive help and counsel. Feelings of belonging and having a place to leave one's worries also provide a way to relax and open ourselves to the experience of peace. Sometimes the knowledge that these are places of comfort and peace presents a person with a location to be free from the troubles of life. These places are expected to help those attending experience and realize peace.

How does everyone else who may not have a set philosophy, religion, or meditative process find peace? If you fall into this group, the answer is that you have to "want it." A person can have a belief structure and still never experience the peace and joy this book tries to explain. Each person is in a different phase of life. Some people struggle on a daily basis to survive, and others are running so fast and so hard that they can't even imagine experiencing a peace that delivers with it a joy that can't quite be explained but only experienced. Even when a person finds themselves in a state of peace and joy, they may say that they don't reside in a state of joy for more than mere moments. A person has to "want" this experience and yet not worry about achieving peace and joy on a whim. Allow yourself to remember those things, times, people, and places that made you happy, maybe even joyful.

Have you ever woken up in the morning and gone outside to see the sunrise or dew on a leaf, and you knew that no matter what happened today it (life) was going to be okay. Imagine that feeling when you experienced a kind of peace, and try to relive it right now. Remember the early morning: the lighting, its smell, the sounds, and how it would feel if you were to touch it. If you take a second to remember the moments that made you happy or calm, don't you feel a little like that right now? You need to remember everything you felt, remember your senses of taste, touch, smell, sound, and all the sights surrounding the event. If it's hard to read and remember, take a moment away from reading and think of those moments of calm and joy and remember everything about that moment until you can almost experience it again in your memory. Remember ...

Remembering the good times tends to help reduce stressors that bother people in emotional, mental and sometimes physiological distress.

The negative person

Avoid people who seem to dwell in difficulty or feel that they are the never-ending victim of life. Or the people who are so negative that it seems they don't ever have a positive thing to say. They might say "hi," but it is never with a smile. These people highlight the idea that everything bad always seems to happen to them. Everyday there is a new drama that presents itself, and often we may even feel that if we see that person today, we will want to walk the other way.

There is a reason that eventually we will want to go the other way or try to hide. It is called "survival." Our lives need to have meaning and a purpose and the energy in which we live life. Unfortunately personalities like this often make people feel as if they suck the life and energy out of us. Why does that person need all of our attention because they chipped a nail or got gunk on their shoe? Talk about a perspective out of whack. These people tend to be toxic to others. Small things do happen that are unpleasant, but most people can put it in the category of "this is not that important."

If the description of a negative person fits your own life, please keep reading. There may be situations and events that have not been resolved from the past. This book hopes to help make life easier and help with the thoughts that may cause some of the negativity. By the end of this book, life may seem a little more positive and relationships a little better.

If it seems that friends are constantly giving negative comments or never have a good thing to say, maybe a new priority should be working toward building friendships with other individuals that have something good to say and a positive demeanor. Positive people are not void of difficulties in life. The only difference between them and others may be the fact that they have a different perspective in life. It is a positive perspective that allows people to be able to "roll with the punches." Find positive people who realize the world does not revolve around them and who have some hope. The more positive the person, the better for friendship.

Often we start to mimic those around us. It is up to each of us to choose or direct ourselves in environments that help us to be the best individual we can be.

A little boy's frustration

There was a little boy just seven years old. He was the shortest child in his class. Academically he had problems reading because he was dyslexic, and unknown to everyone else, his eyesight was very poor. He was overweight, "hearty" as his grandfather would describe him, so the boy was picked on ruthlessly by the school bullies.

One day, he went to school and took a test. He kept asking what the text was saying, and the substitute teacher responded that reading was part of the test. Normally the regular teacher would read it because she knew that he was diagnosed with dyslexia and tended to mix up words. After the exam, his class had snack time. Then the substitute wrote vocabulary on the board and asked the children to write the sentence using each word. He couldn't see what she was writing so he asked to come and look at the board closely. After he came up to the board a few more times, the substitute lost her patience and told him to wait until all the words were up and to write what he could. Since he was not fast enough he had to stay in for recess. At this point he was frustrated and starting to get angry at the injustice of not being able to go play during recess.

After school, the bullies decided they were going to pick on him as they called him "chubby and dumb." When he tried to walk with his older sister so the bullies would leave him alone, she decided instead to stay with her friends. He kept trying to catch up with her group only to be turned away and taunted by the boys all the way home.

He had had it. The teacher picked on him, he missed recess, the bullies got on his last nerve, and his sister didn't even help. Just one more thing and he was going to explode.

When he went into the door of the house, his mom was on the phone and his sister went upstairs to do whatever it is that girls do. He slammed the door to get a little attention, and he wanted to tell his mom how his sister kept ditching him. When his mom got off the phone, she called to her son in a stern voice to ask what he thought he was doing to slam the door so loud. Even *Mom* was mad at him. So doing the only thing he could do, he threw his bag to the floor and started yelling about his sister and the day. But before he could go much further, his mother told him to stop and stand in the corner and calm down and think about the way he was acting.

He did as he was told, stomping the whole way to the corner. When he approached corner, he saw his dog laying there. He told the dog to move, and it didn't. So he kicked the dog. It was the dog's fault for being there he told himself. The dog yelped, and the mother came to the dog's aid with the look of worry and annoyance. He knew it was wrong to kick the dog, but everyone was picking on him and the dog was the only thing that he could pick on.

After he was able to compose himself as good as a seven-year-old with a temper could, he told his mom of what had been going on in the day. He told her about the teacher, the test, blackboard, recess, bullies, and his sister. After he explained his day with tears in his eyes, the anger and frustration started to drain out of him. He was angry, but he felt better now and was sorry for kicking the dog. The intensity and duration of emotion throughout the day led to him making poor decisions.

When the boy had finally told his story and let go of his negative emotions he was able to relax. Young children have not yet learned that these situations need to be dealt with proactively. Simply telling the substitute that seeing the board is hard or that his teacher usually reads the test to him would have made the class better. Unlike adults, this boy did not learn many lessons in life yet, and this event would be the catalyst for his mom teaching him to become more proactive and a little more outspoken, but also how to do so without getting in trouble. She will teach him mechanisms that reduced his stress. Most of all, he learned that telling someone the happenings and events of the day that make a person upset and frustrated to a point of tears feels good afterward and makes the rest of the day easier.

Just venting

To reduce stress on a daily basis, find a friend or family member to whom you can vent. This means talking out those events of the day that seem to carry with you throughout the day. Just remember that the person you are venting to is not the person who caused you this grief. Sometimes instead of getting the situation off our chest or immediate memory, we have a tendency to relive the anger or frustration of the moment. Vent but don't direct any negative emotion to your confidant; they are human, too. As adults we need to be able to vent without inflicting harm on the listener. Venting allows us to clean our emotional slate. Speaking with a friend might even help us to improve the situation next time by sharing ideas and examples of what they have done in similar situations.

Usually when we vent, we are able to move on with the rest of the day. Sometimes it would be good to get the emotion out of our system quickly so we can resolve to move forward more positively. With our head clear of emotional negativity and a more positive perspective, we can react properly to situational stressors. Anger, sadness, or frustration only clouds our judgment. When we act out or make decisions in a fog of emotion and when our perspective is pushed outside of rational thinking, we have a tendency to "kick the dog"—pick on the smaller, weaker, or lower ranking person or thing in the vicinity.

Most people have experienced other colleagues or family members somehow punishing them for something they didn't do. Often the action can be traced to outside stressors being placed on the person, and the stress will be shared by acting out or causing stress toward others. Remember that the next time you start to yell at others when they have done nothing wrong.

Voice your frustration, or say you're having a bad day. Try to avoid making others have a bad day also. Those around you will appreciate it and also avoid annoying you further. Most people aren't out to get you, so being honest about your problems and asking for help is often the right thing to do.

Get it off your mind

Sometimes, we may not feel that we can vent to anyone at work or at home but need to release the negative energy. Another way to reduce stress in the event you may not have someone you can vent to is to write it down in a journal or on a piece of paper and then shred it. A confetti shredder can be a very healthy thing to own for a person in this situation. Sometimes the physical act of writing then shredding the negative things in your life provides a means to get out the frustration. Often the handwriting may look atrocious, but who cares? Let it out, shred it, and then move on to doing something you do like or that is productive and not negatively affecting you.

Fear and guilt

How often do we spend our time in fear or guilt for past actions and experiences? We end up reliving the past as though it just occurred, and then we realize we did not resolve our own feelings on the issue. What needs to be said is "Let it go."

Fear and guilt are the two major feelings that hold us back and drag us down. Letting go of the fear and guilt allow us to live for the moment, plan for the future, and stay in a better place mentally. We have to live in the immediacy of the situation of our lives and allow ourselves to experience a life rich in the good and positive now.

Many say "greed is the root to all evil." This statement can be debated because there are reasons for a person's greed. Instead, let's postulate that fear of poverty, fear of the lack of social respect, fear of becoming a nobody, fear of rejection, fear of not living up to our own or someone else's standard becomes the source for "greed." Fear is a great motivator toward protection, and too much fear becomes the source of poor choices and actions. Like all things, there is a good reason for fear, and occasionally it is motivator for good. When we live our lives in fear, it becomes a negative motivator and can often be the beginning of our demise: fear of failure, fear of being alone, and fear of being poor. When we make decisions based on these fears, we start to make poor decisions that most often become a source of guilt.

When we live in guilt, we seem to be stunted from becoming better people and from learning from the mistakes of our past. Instead we start to relive the moment that caused the guilt. That action usually results from a fear that we had perceived and acted on. Basically the combination of fear and guilt becomes a vicious circle that returns to fear and guilt and manifests itself usually in poor decisions and negativity.

A police story

Let us take a look at our police force. They are often underpaid and underappreciated, yet they are some of the most important civil servants in our society. They deserve a great amount of respect. They help people every day and are held to a very high standard. Talk about a group of people that must deal with the unknown and the thought that the next suspect might be the one who blows their head off. How do they deal with the immense amount of stress and the unknown? Police who are well trained have a clear knowledge of what is expected of them and how they are to assess the situation that is at hand. Their training helps reduce the fear of the unknown.

The fact of the matter is that they cannot ignore all the unknown and danger in any given situation. Instead of letting fear overtake them and the discomfort of the unknown distract them, training and experience aids them. They think and concentrate on the situation and understand the surroundings and the possible scenarios that might occur in any given situation. Training and knowledge in one's own abilities becomes the stabilizing factor in a dynamic and unknown situation.

When fear creeps in to the point that rational thinking and training go by the wayside, accidental shootings where there are no weapons in the possession of a suspect come to bear. Why did the shooting happen? It's an odd situation, the possibly fatal and unknown actions of the suspect with a weapon, the fear of losing one's life in the field and leaving the family at home without a parent or a spouse. The idea that this is the end, and it is me or them. This is not training or expertise coming into play. This is fear.

Fear clouds our judgment and our ability to take the situation and analyze it. Some may say you can't analyze this situation. True, sometimes things happen so fast that a decision has to be made in the snap of a moment. Many police officers would say that a kill shot is not what you are going for unless the immediate moment proves to be the deciding factor between the life and death of the officer and the civilians around them. In the event of an accidental shooting, there is usually guilt that creeps in. There may be time for investigation and a break for the officer, but often debriefing and psychological evaluation is done. This is not only to make sure that the officer was in his/her right mind at the time of the shooting, but in order to assess the ability of the officer to continue at their duty and make sure that they can deal with the guilt that often comes afterward.

Guilt will often take hold on a person to the point of making them paralyzed from being able to work in the field and to use a firearm in the future when the shot is necessary. People in general do not like to make mistakes and even less like to hurt people. Police often go into the job to help people and make a difference. There are some exceptions, but the majority of police are good and well intentioned civil servants. Accidents happen, but the guilt involved in an accidental or needless death often creates a situation for the officer that may make being on the streets no longer an option.

Fear of the unknown, of change, of consequences for actions we are not so clear on, can be troublesome. How many kinds of fears are there? More than we can easily count. There are fears that protect us, like the fear of crossing the street with our eyes closed. This is a good fear because it protects our life. The fear that someone may pull a weapon on a police officer unexpectedly is a good fear, but one that needs to be quelled in order to make measured decisions that reduce risk of accidental firearms discharge. Most first responders and emergency room medical staff have similar life or death decisions to make based on the situation and the immediacy of the needs of the people they are trying to help. They too have fears that have to be quelled by training and experience or else someone may die. The key to facing fear is to trust our knowledge and the experience we have will make each new experience easier and the fear will lessen.

Fear of the unknown and change

Why do we not like change? It is the fear of the unknown. When confronted with the need to change or become more flexible with our daily routines or expectations, do we say "bring it on" or "oh no"? How we react is based often on our level of fear. Our reactions and our understanding of the consequences could engulf us in fear and/or guilt, and then our understanding of where we are in the midst of this new dynamic can give us a sense of loss of control.

Often we become people of habit. We like knowing what to expect. When we wake up, we like knowing where the bathroom is. We like our normal waking-up routine. When we head off to school, work, or play, we like to have an idea what we will be doing, and when we come home, we want to know where we are going to sleep. At the core of "needing to know" these things is the real need to know that we have shelter, food, clothing, purpose, and some level of control in our lives. When we become truly adverse to change is when others can end up controlling us. Learning to adjust and take on situations of change affords us the ability to have more control of ourselves. We can't control the actions of others or at least shouldn't try to manipulate others in hopes of controlling them. We can only control ourselves. If a person finds themselves in a position where change has not been inserted into their life and they like it that way and do not want anything to change, then it might be a good idea to change things up themselves before life does it for them. Something has got to give. If a person owns a home and doesn't do any maintenance on it, eventually something is going to change and usually at the most inopportune time.

We can control the initiator of change and the key element of this is being aware of ourselves and the environment around us. Change hits hard when we least expect it, and when it is demanded of us. When we expect change, we become prepared to expect "something" different. By our preparation, we also become less fearful of what to expect. If we initiate the change, we control its direction and most of the time its outcome. If we observe subtle changes in our workplace, global economic situations, and neighborhood activities, then we often won't be surprised at the new policies at work, global currency changes, or the new speed bumps in our neighborhood.

If one day we went to get gasoline for our car and gas prices went up fifty cents, we would certainly be upset. On the other hand if we had been paying attention to our environment and the world around us, we would have had some warning by the fact that a tax was passed in order to improve transportation infrastructure. The tax idea was approved because of the need for mass transit and improvements in road conditions. We may not like the decision or reasons and we can still wish the price was lower, but knowing the reasons keeps us from undue stress. No one likes paying more for gas, but it doesn't mean we have to get upset about it and have it ruin our day.

Change happens, and our knowledge shapes our perception of the events and often our reticence toward change. The resulting personal response to change will also allow us to remain calm and happy more than upset or angry.

Fear of rejection

Fear of rejection, being alone, not liking what we see in the mirror, fears of talking with people, fear of the workplace and letting people into our life encompasses the fear of rejection. Often it is in this area that we make the most common mistakes, and this is the area of fear that occurs in our daily lives. Think about your own life. When is it that you have ever told a fib, lied, or pretended to be something you are not? Was it at work when you didn't know the answer to something that you thought someone in your position should know? Was it on a date when you said you did something that sounded impressive when you did not? Why don't you try to go to that new restaurant? Is it because you are afraid you won't know what to order, or because you may not have enough money to pay for the menu items? Is it because of money or fear of looking dumb or poor? If you went in, looked at the menu and found out it is too pricey, what is wrong with the idea of walking out before ordering and telling the waiter or maître d' that you changed your mind? How afraid are you when it comes to what people think about you? We all have a level of fear of rejection or judgment about what the other person thinks of us. The more we care about the person and the greater we want our relationships to be, the more we feel we have at stake. It is our fears that tend to drive us to make the mistakes that would end a relationship before it even gets started.

Why are we focusing so much on relational fear and guilt? The reason for choosing this topic is that most of our fear in life revolves around people and the need of acceptance and companionship. Why is it so hard for some guys to ask a girl out on a date, while others will ask more readily? Fear of rejection.

We all want to believe we are better than we really are. While this may be true and something to work toward, we often do not realize that who we are right now is still pretty good. Even when we continue to better ourselves, often we are our own worst critic. Those who do not see any error in themselves tend to be narcissistic and often are truly lonely or significantly delusional. Admitting to ourselves our own weaknesses can open us to the fear that everyone else sees the same weaknesses in us. Fear of rejection is the largest fear factor for the common everyday person.

When we go to work, we want to be appreciated for our work. No criticism is much more preferred over constructive criticism, even though we can improve with constructive criticism. Many of us feel a level of rejection when someone finds it necessary to criticize us. When we improve on the area criticized our work will be more appreciated and less likely to be rejected in the future. Try not to take the constructive criticism personally and you won't be prone to getting so upset in the face of the criticism. If the criticism is not valid and someone is just trying to be mean, you will be able to identify the difference if you listen to the criticism with an open mind. It is then possible to go through the day better off and not having to reflect on someone else's poor judgment to criticize something not valid.

Understand that fear of rejection from the people around us means that we have something at stake. What do we think we have stake? Our egos, self-image, maybe we are afraid that people will see beyond our façade and into our insecurities. Instead of worrying that people are paying that much attention to you, consider that everyone else has some level of that same fear. We all have insecurities; instead of focusing on them, let's focus on simply seeing others as potential friends. Say "hello" and wear a smile. Many people are attracted to people who smile because often it is a friend or a kind person who will share a smile with a stranger. It is harder to be mean or judgmental when we look for kindness in people. Often it makes it harder for others to negatively judge us if we smile at them first.

Trust issues and fear

What happens when you find out that your date or budding relationship lied to you? Does that trust fall because of the deception? Often when we are in relationships, trust is one of the hardest parts of the relationship to build. Often this is due to fear of being hurt, used and abused. Maybe because we have seen examples in other people's lives, or even worse, we have experienced these events in our own lives. Therefore, each level of deception becomes a larger reason not to become so vested in the relationship from the beginning.

Is it our own lies, disappointments, and fear of having relationships, yet caring so much about losing it, that makes us sabotage ourselves and force each relationship to fail? Do we find that in relationships we are our worst enemies? We create the self-fulfilling prophecy. Fear of commitment and being "attached" often comes from our own knowledge of relationships such as our parents, possibly a divorce, betrayal of our best friend, or even our past with a pet that died at an inopportune time when we were learning to create relationships. Our past can come to build our fears and guilt.

Have we lied to make ourselves look good and then later found out we want to deepen our relationship with a person only to feel like we have to keep up the lie? We do not want them to think poorly about us, and in so doing our web of lies become a web of guilt. Then we find that coming clean is so hard that we end the relationship in fear that the truth will cause our rejection. Because of the lie, we will tend to bury our feelings. Then hurt would ensue not only to our relationship but to our very being and how we see ourselves.

Do you see how fear and guilt create a cycle that deepens in its intensity until the concept and idea of escape seems almost impossible? Those who never lie and deal with the possibility of rejection of our true self do not understand how someone can fall into a vicious cycle of fear, guilt, and fear. They do not understand because they are more afraid of lying. They possibly have understood early on that lying is uglier and more harmful than the rejection that comes from the truth. Finding a real friend who understands the weaknesses you have and accepting the possibility that you might be rejected early on is easier than coming closer in a relationship based on a lie. It is this dynamic of fear and guilt that ultimately causes our own loneliness.

Sometimes, those who have had painful events happen in their past can't live without the distrust of others and cannot experience the ability to trust anyone. These lessons learned help form how we treat others and experience the world around us. Sometimes these experiences had such an effect on us that we put blame and distrust on people who have not earned either. Not being able to trust people is a bad thing. Yes, there are bad people in the world. We would even venture to say there are flat out "evil" people in the world. People who have lost their sense of humanity deserve neither trust nor the right to roam amongst the public with freedom to harm others. While saying all this, we should venture to consider that most people in this world are generally good. When you approach people with this attitude, you will also see the better of the person. A person who has been so scarred by the "evil" aspects of the world and have been so changed by those people find themselves almost incapable of trusting others and often become alone. They will create invisible walls against letting other people get to know them. This is not good.

Events of the past

If you have not dealt with the events of the past to the point that you are in a state of paranoia or distrust everyone even though they have not "earned" that distrust, please seek out a way to deal with it. Psychologists and psychiatrists are trained in these areas. Finding a person with good credentials, references and experience in the field of psychology, psychiatry, or counseling is important. The first time a person meets such counselors, it may seem odd. The ability to trust them may be difficult, but try. The main point is to deal with what has happened and move forward. You want to live life. Start living it even while you are trying to deal with it.

Do you have any sort of friend who has always been there, but you have not trusted them for fear that they will hurt you? Well, have you told them you appreciate them? Do they already sense the reason you are the way you are because of the past? Most of the time these individuals also have had "stuff" they have had to deal with, and that is why the two of you get along. Venture to share your experiences with them. Maybe they have a clue of how to help. Yes, it is a risk to trust a friend, but maybe the friendship needs to become closer or maybe the truth may very well set you free.

Seeking professional help

There is a lot of deserved respect for professional, educated, and experienced psychologists and psychiatrists, but not all of us can afford their services and maybe our own personal fears still get in the way of seeking their help. The younger generations have grown up in a culture where the idea of going to a psychologist or psychiatrist seems as normal as going to the dentist. There isn't this idea of a negative stigma. Once, not so long ago, unwed mothers would face serious shame for the fact that they had engaged in sexual conduct and had a child out of wedlock. Now, such things occur and some quite intentionally without any want of marriage, and society doesn't hold the same views of the past. The same is true for professional psychological help.

Our parents and grandparents grew up in a time that going to psychological professionals was a sign of weakness. They may have been discriminated socially and professionally if others found out. That old "stigma" is no longer the situation. Those who now seek professional help are looked at similarly to someone going to the dentist for a tooth ache. It is better to get the issue fixed or at least dealt with than to keep dealing with the pain and not seek help. Some would even venture to say that if you don't seek help then you really are crazy. Who wants to deal with the pain alone? Sometimes if we deal with the pain, it goes away or at least it does not hurt as much. Emotional pain can be debilitating. Overly strong negative memories can be debilitating as well. Why would anyone want that handicap? We deserve to have these events behind us. Realize that no matter how awful and life changing the event, it does not have to rule your life.

If an especially bad event has occurred in your life and you feel like you relive that event over and over, I beseech you to seek professional help. Those who have experienced war or had to make decisions that affected another person's life, or those who have been affected by the poor choice of others, such as molestation, rape, sexual, physical, psychological, and other abuses, may have had an experience so burned into their memory that the experience is relived in all its emotion and intensity. This reliving with the psychological and sometimes physiological memory can be referred to as Post Traumatic Stress Disorder (PTSD). PTSD can create disassociative behavior that can affect our hours, days, months, and years, and if not dealt with, the rest of our lives.

It is one thing to have these events relived in dreams, but some people relive these events in their waking hours. Sometimes there will be a trigger to these negative events, and then the person with PTSD will seem to be elsewhere. The conversation or the activity that is going around this individual will fall to the background, and the event will be relived as though it is happening all over again. Forgetting the here and now will pull them away from the reality of what is happening around them. It is like being stuck in a memory and the whole time the person is reliving the past while totally forgetting the present location or situation. In time, these events of disassociation with the present occur more often, and the individual can slowly or more quickly no longer know the reality of the present. They react to the current surroundings as if the negative events are still happening. It is for this reason that a person in this situation must seek professional help from certified psychiatrists. These are people with medical degrees as well as clinical hours counseling people. They have the ability to assist through sessions of counseling as well as any physiological chemical issues.

Post-partum depression

Post-partum depression is an issue of many new mothers but there are free sources of assistance in this area. This form of depression is often short term, but can present itself much longer due to more permanent changes to the woman's body chemistry. Be honest and open with your doctor about how you are doing after the birth. Often, your OB/GYN can refer you to people who work in this field. Assistance in this area is often covered by many insurance carriers, and there are free clinics and other sources of help if needed.

If you can't afford to speak with a psychiatrist or psychologist, please seek a confidant, pastor, or special friend to talk about the negative memory or event. When singular events are the issue, the event, though serious and sometimes life altering, can be reduced to memories with time and without the need of specialized professional help. If you are in a state of unnecessary worry or dealing with the loss of family, friend, or a pet (which can feel like both friend and family), finding another person to talk to will help.

If coping with a loss of a special someone, seek out the person or people who have had a similar loss but have come out of it all right. Sometimes asking people who have gone through a similar crisis and finding out how they survived it helps to create a sense of support and connection.

Escaping the physical source of misery

If the source of your misery is living with you in your home, you need to consider your options; agreeing to separate, kick them out, or leaving yourself so that you can move forward with your life. This is easily stated and sometimes much harder to do. Some people, once they figure out they are in an abusive relationship can just say, "Okay, i'm gone," and leave. For others this is not the case because our lives can be so complicated, especially when it comes to your own family. Please seek help in the form of shelters (women's, battery, physical abuse, domestic abuse, etc.), legal authorities such as the local police stations or trusted friends and relatives. Internet resources as well as phone books have information about help lines for abuse and crises centers. Contact these centers and ask them what you need to do to get out of the situation. Leave the location of the abuse if possible as soon as possible. Whether you are a child, adult, female or male, abuse is abuse and it is wrong. Leave the situation through non-violent and legal means. Once you are free and safe, seek help from counselors and psychological professionals to discuss your feelings and deal with the hurt and anger.

Understanding that the past is the past and yet it is a part of us, for better or worse, gives us a perspective that helps us look at the present more objectively. Do what you can to resolve that major event that has such a hold on you. If you have negative events in your mind but your life is not so revolved around them, then everything else stated in this book is attainable, if not now, in time. If your life does revolve around negative events, please read on but realize that these events need to be resolved. Whether it is through counseling, with the help of ones who love you, or just your own determination to replace the poor memory with one that is more encouraging, attainment of daily peace that becomes a lasting reality is a goal worth pursuing.

The past is a part of us, and the lessons learned help us to become who we are. We can take those "bad" experiences, learn the lessons, and direct them so that we can be happier in our lives currently. We make those experiences serve a better cause by taking charge of those memories. At the same time we overcome any level of subservient tendencies we have to those negative events in our lives. This allows us to then place those events in memory but not have to relive them. How we use the lessons learned and incorporate them into our lives is a whole other story. Lessons learned allow us to become wiser, and the experience helps us to better understand people and the world around us.

How we incorporate the information also forms our perceptions, which in essence become our reality. This can be debated, considering there is a whole area of philosophy dedicated to the area of what makes us who we are. We are going to skip the philosophical debate and say that we ascribe to the idea that who we are is in part the result of our experiences. Our natural and/or learned tendencies toward incorporating the information we gain from our observation, education, and experience only make us wiser and better people.

Chapter 3
Opening Yourself to
Peace and Joy

The opportunities to find peace and joy surround us every day. Choosing to seek peace and joy in our lives helps us to better see the opportunities we are given. The air we breathe can seem sweet and refreshing. The water we drink can fill our thirst. Food can be not only a means of satisfying our hunger but also a way to savor the variety of flavors that are offered and felt with our taste buds. Our pets make us feel needed. The softness of their fur reminds us that touch is so important. Our partner can teach us what it means to share life and joy even amongst the challenges of life. A shower or stream of water that cleanses the grime and negativity of a day away is refreshing, soothing and calm. The moments of silent nothingness can be a brief retreat from the cares of a full day. Opportunities to enjoy life surround us every day, but we need to be aware of them. We need to want to see them around us.

Take care to remember those special moments that are not always in our daily lives. These things include the weddings, births, and graduations of those in our life. The special joys that our neighbors, families and friends share become ever more important when we treasure them. Take the moment to relish these times, for they happen just briefly. These larger events often feed our imaginations, dreams, and hopes for the future and are a fuel for those things that keep us going in the hardest of times.

Our experiences, good or bad, are a part of us and help us become who we are today. The mistakes we make in life are all a part of the learning process. Making peace with our experiences and accepting the lessons we learn help to create more of a flow in our daily lives. There will be days when everything falls into place, and other days when nothing seems to work the way you think it should. When bad things happen, we deal with it and move on. We can allow ourselves to relish the small victories and celebrate our successes. If we allow ourselves to ride the waves of life, we might be able to learn to have a little more fun with it. When we fight the daily lessons and events in our life and chose to not like change or at least not deal with it, then life becomes more of a chore and more readily a person starts to feel as if the world is against them.

Have you ever known someone who constantly seems to have terrible things happen to them? Maybe they complain about how horrible life is every day and how nothing good ever happens to them? Things seem to always be catastrophic, and the world is out to get them? Maybe you are the person who feels this way.

Ask yourself, does this individual deal with life as it comes? Do they experience life or do they try to avoid almost everything that happens to them? Do they procrastinate instead of dealing with problems and then complain or blame the world? Is everything bad everybody else's fault? Does there always need to be reason, fault, or blame for everything?

Forgetting the bad is easier if you have dealt with it. Stop finding blame or fault. "Bad things happen. Deal with it." These sentences are nothing new. We have heard them from family, friends, books, media, and even games. Dealing with it may seem hard, but it is totally worth it so that we can move on. If someone cuts us off on the highway, do we curse at them and continue to criticize their driving, or do we say a short expletive, get it out of our system, and then get back to focusing on our own driving? Some of us may choose to get mad and try to get even. When we hyper focus on that event, often we tend to become the offenders of such rude and downright dangerous behavior. How we "deal with it" determines our ability to come to terms with whatever "it" is. Finding peace sometimes means making it for ourselves. Feeling the pain, hurt, and anger, then choosing to let it go is a part of living a life focused on peace. Whenever you can find that peace, you can experience the joy and live a generally happy life.

It is how we remember these events that can predict how they will be placed in our lives and their effect on us in the long term. Don't cling to short-term injury, sad, angry, or negative times. Life deals out enough major events that we do not need to hold onto small stuff. It can be said that peace is "knowing that no matter what happens in the world, our lives will go on in spite of it." Often the word "world" does not mean the Planet Earth but the micro world of our sphere of experience and the surroundings of our lives within our society, work, and family. The more you think in the macro sense of the state, country, and global world, the easier it is to take your experiences and put them into a healthier perspective.

"That's life"

Everyone has heard the term "that's life," or the multitude of variations. Look, we don't live in a bubble, and bad things happen to us regardless of how we see the world. No matter what happens, we won't be able to control everything. In those times the thought of trying to think or be in a place of peace seems impossible. It would have to be said that for the short term maybe it is impossible. I urge you to mourn and grieve or get angry if you must, but try to keep that period of time as short as possible. Take these times as your momentary setbacks.

Try to see any humor in a situation and any good that can come out of it. If this too seems impossible, then search for the strength within yourself to push beyond the situation and understand that the only thing you can control sometimes is how you respond to it.

The Tennessee Flood of 2010

There was a flood in the area of Nashville, and a lot of people lost their homes that did not have flood insurance. They had to rebuild with no money and yet continue to pay a mortgage for a home that could not be lived in. The pain and the hurt was so raw, and the evidence of their grief stared them in their face. Some decided to mourn every day of rebuilding their homes and their lives. Others were grateful just to be alive. The situations were the same, the only difference was the perspective. One was wallowing in self-pity, and the other had a sense of loss, but not total loss. In having this perspective, they were also allowing themselves more control of the situation. Using the few resources available, maybe just a cell phone or laptop, they were able to seek out help. Connecting with charities and aid agencies, they took care of their immediate needs and then quickly focused on rebuilding. In not having the situation control them, they could control their response and ultimately the resolution of the situation.

Sometimes our very responses to horrible events can be the segue to our healing and an opportunity for personal growth. Times of hardship often bring out the strength and generosity that we often don't know we are capable of or we have forgotten about. Though the events are horrible, we can become better people, stronger in conviction and renewed in the scope of our own abilities. Life doesn't always dish out what we expect, want, or deserve. All we can do is strive to live life the best we can and make a difference when we can.

Our response to significant events in life or just dealing with the day-to-day issues requires action on our part. If we don't eat or drink we die, so we eat and drink. If we remain in bed and do not go to work, the store, or just get up and out, time will pass us by. Time is the most valuable asset we have. We sometimes waste our time and get neither rest nor results. Time cannot be saved like money, and there isn't a rewind button to have a redo.

We need to deal with matters at hand, as they happen. When we procrastinate or try to not see what responsibilities we are beholden to, then things tend to get worse. The idea that "a stitch in time saves nine" is a good one, for if we fix problems and situations as they happen, our personal effort to resolve them will be lessened. If not solved immediately, often the issues can spiral out of control. If we can resolve a situation immediately, we do not have to give it any further thought or worry. When we procrastinate, the situation will fester in the back of our mind until we decide to deal with it.

Car story

There was a successful lawyer in the Washington, D.C., metropolitan area who was absolutely brilliant at her job. She practiced many areas of law in the tri-state district and she enjoyed litigation. She was single and work consumed her life. She loved what she did, so most of the time work didn't feel like work. Her associates and staff members were closer to her than her own biological family, and she often spent her time off with them as well.

After one of her successful days in court, the office had an impromptu dinner party at a restaurant. The conversation ranged from how much work they had done to the various cars that the people owned. The topic of getting the oil changed every three months or three thousand miles came up. One person mentioned they had synthetic oil so they had their oil changed every six months. Everybody seemed to mention how often they got their car worked on. When someone turned to our successful attorney she looked at the group somewhat baffled. She stated that she always had problems with cars and was not sure why. She then went on to say she is not so good at getting the oil changed and had just bought the vehicle maybe six months ago. At this, several people started to tell her that her car was definitely due for an oil change and maybe that is why she kept having problems with the vehicle. She then told the group she would take care of it next week, and the conversation turned to other topics.

The very next day her check engine light came on. She was annoyed to see it lit up given the conversation she had just the night before and decided that she should probably schedule to get her oil changed soon. In her busy life, a week passed quickly and then two. Then one month later on a hot and humid day, her car decided not to start. She was not happy and had to find another way to get to work. When she told her assistant that her car wouldn't start, the assistant mentioned the conversation they had a month ago about getting the oil changed. She had forgotten she was planning to get it worked on. She had to leave work early for her auto club to tow it to the closest automotive shop.

The auto shop attendant asked what the problem was, but all she could say was it did not start. He continued to ask the normal questions of year, make, model, and plate number, and all she knew was the make and model of the vehicle. He then asked if she had brought her vehicle to them before. With pride she smiled and said that she has never had to take her car in anywhere. "This is a new car so I don't know what the problem could be." Afterward filling out the computerized form, the automotive technician asked her to show him her vehicle so he could get the rest of the information from the vehicle into the computer so the technicians could get working on it.

When he exited the building and looked out into the parking lot, he saw what he assumed was the lady's vehicle. He frowned momentarily, and the lawyer being observant caught his facial expression. She turned to him and asked him what was wrong. He looked at her and replied, "When did you buy your car?" "About six months ago." He then asked," Did the dealership say it was new when you bought it?" In response she said, "Yes." Well, Miss, "Your vehicle is over a year old, almost two if I'm correct."

She stood stunned because she perceived that she had gotten ripped off by the dealer, but then thought for a moment longer before saying anything further. She started toward the car and looked at her paperwork, and found herself to have forgotten when she purchased her vehicle. She thought for a moment further and found herself surprised about how fast time flies. Then she verified the year with the technician, and he had it worked on as she got into her rental car and drove off. The next day, she got a call at work from the technician. He told her that her engine had seized and asked when was the last time she had gotten an oil change. To her embarrassment she said "never" and remembered the conversation she had just weeks before. Then he asked if she had ever noticed the engine light come on, and she didn't want to answer. He then said they wanted to know so they could fix the service engine light if they had to. At this, she said it worked but she was just so busy and it was too much of a hassle. The cost of repairs on her vehicle was hefty. Since then, even though she felt too busy to get an oil change, she schedules it on her calendar, and she immediately gets her car checked whenever the service engine light comes on.

Have you ever tried to forget something bad that happened to you? It may not have been something serious, but you just didn't want to deal with it at the time. Instead it kept bugging you in the recesses of your mind, and maybe you didn't even get to sleep well that night. When you finally dealt with the situation, did you ask yourself, "Why didn't I just deal with it then? It wouldn't have bothered me so much." In general, most people will be able to relate to this, and yet we still put off dealing with issues. Sometimes we don't want to deal with hurt or disappointment. The feeling that we can't deal with one more thing is a horrible position to be in. Some problems in life are too much for anyone to handle alone, but we can handle most of our problems if we only improve our attitude and the approach to solving it.

Handling events and issues as they occur will in the long run reduce your stress, and you will gain back the wasted time that occurs because of worrying about what you have put off. What happens when you leave dishes on the table or in the sink instead of quickly rinsing the plate and putting it in the dishwasher? Often the food hardens, and later you will have to work much harder to scrape the plate. Often this wastes time, water, energy, and, in the end, money. It is said that time is money. The most expensive thing a person can waste is time, yet we often waste so much of it. Procrastination is often a hindrance to finding peace and joy, because with procrastination comes worry and anxiety. Deal with issues as they happen so you do not linger in worry and you will experience peace and joy as it comes.

Is your glass half full or half empty?

This comment follows the idea that people "see the glass as half empty or half full." What does that mean? Well, when thirsty, a person would want the glass full, but the glass has only half that much. Where do you find yourself? Do you feel that the glass is half full or half empty? I would venture to say that as long as there is something in our cup and we know where we can refill it, most of us don't care. So what does it matter if our cup is half full or half empty? It matters, because the difference is the way we look at it and everything else in life. In our cup of life, do we see opportunities and potential, even in the midst of hardship? Or because of our burdens, do we feel like we are holding on by a thread? The difference is not how life is treating you, but how we choose to look at life.

All of us are capable of surviving and have the potential to even flourish. Maybe it is our survival instincts that make us think we need more even when we are doing just fine. Even a good life is not easy. If we let the events of our daily life determine our outlook, most of us will be in that half-empty frame of mind. Those among us who do flourish make that extra effort to see the potential in each opportunity and each new day. Even when we feel at our limits, we can make the effort to look beyond the obstacles. By doing this, we will see the challenge for what it is. We all need a little help every once in a while. We might get it in a friend, relative, or maybe a kind stranger. Often just enough help is given to give us that little boost we need. All we need to do is see that help is there if only we open our eyes, ears, and heart. When we are in a half-empty mindset, we may ignore the help when it is offered and our cup stays that way for a long time.

Peace resides in a place where perspective is positive yet still grounded in reality. Reality is formed by the perspective we choose to see it from. Choose a positive perspective so that: reality is palatable, peace possible and joy becomes a reality.

Are you the "half full" or "half empty" kind of person? Can we truly choose? No one said the choice would be easy, only that the choice should be made. No one can make that choice for us. It is up to the individual. Others may help us to live that choice, but we are the ones who have to decide. If you are your own worst critic and you have problems realizing that you are important and deserve happiness, start talking more with those individuals who make you happy or feel worthwhile. If no one has said it to you recently, you are truly important and worthy of love and being loved. You deserve to know that your presence on this Earth is so important that it would be wrong to waste it being sad for yourself.

Every person affects another person, so every person is important. Choosing a life looking and yearning for its positive aspects is a more attractive trait to those around us and maybe even ourselves.

Perspective

The broken down car

One day a man was driving back to Maryland from Washington, D.C., in the evening hours. This young man had to drive through a tough stretch of neighborhood. As he was driving, he saw a middle-aged black man dressed in a T-shirt and jeans looking underneath the hood of his car. This young man pulled to the side of the street to help the older gentleman.

After realizing that he needed more than a jump start, the older gentleman said he could not afford a tow until his next pay day. Feeling compassion for the distressed older gentleman, the young man went to an ATM, took out a couple hundred, and gave his contact information and address to the older man so he could send the money back when he got paid. The young man waited until the older man made a call from a pay phone, and the older gentleman said that he would wait by his car until the tow truck came. After the older gentleman was settled at his vehicle, the young man left feeling he had made a difference that evening.

When he came home much later than his wife expected, she asked him what happened. After he finished telling his story, his wife had a deep frown on her face and looked very concerned. He beamed with his feeling of accomplishment in helping someone, and instead of her looking happy or proud for his good deed, she looked upset and was almost mad. He turned to her and asked her what was wrong. She told him that the guy was probably selling drugs and was standing there so the police wouldn't think he was loitering; she knew that the police tried not to stop at any stretch of that area for fear of their lives. There had been a string of robberies at the ATM where people had hundreds stolen from them, and the people had not been caught. Then she was worried that now a complete stranger had their information and knows how nice and possibly gullible her husband was. She was sure they were out a couple hundred dollars, and they needed the money to last.

For the older man, it seemed to him that he had a bad day and his car had to break down in the worst part of town. He was a black man, in a bad part of town with his car broken right off the exit to a main highway at night. He did not own a cell phone, and he knew he was probably in trouble. Police did not come to this part of town unless there was a specific call to go there, and too many people were too smart to stop in this part of town unless they were the bad guys to begin with. He didn't want to flag another car down because there had been a rash of muggings, beating, and murders in this part of town.

As he started to have this sinking feeling he was in trouble, he thought to pray for a miracle. A young man pulled up with Maryland license plates. This older gentleman was a bit worried but held his composure while saying a small prayer under his breath. This young man asked him if he needed a jump start and started to try to help. The older gentleman was pretty sure that was not the case but let the young man help. Like he expected, the car still did not work but neither gentlemen knew for certain what was wrong with the car.

The older man said to the younger gentleman that the car was old and had been giving him trouble. He was hoping it would last just a little longer. The young gentleman asked if he belonged to an automotive club, and the older man shook his head "no." The older gentleman said he did not even get paid until the following week and he couldn't even get it towed. The young man looked at him with compassion and concern and said, "If I can get to an ATM, I can loan you some money and you can pay me back when you get paid."

The older gentleman was already surprised for the help of this stranger, and then he offered money to him and gave him all his contact information. He once thought that only crooks would stop, no one would help, and yet a young white man stopped in the worse part of town to help middle-aged black man and loan him money.

Well, the older gentleman took the money and information with full intent to pay the young man back. After the tow truck dropped off the vehicle and the older gentleman, he told his story to his wife. She was surprised the young man did not get any further information from the older gentleman. Later that week, the older gentleman was preparing his check to send to the helpful young man and looked for the address. Too much his distress he could not find the paper so he asked his wife. She said he should check his pockets. He then realized his pants had been washed. When he pulled at his pockets, pieces of paper came out with ink that had obviously run through the paper and the pants pocket. He had lost the young man's information and was never able to pay him back.

Instead the man chose to take the money and help a nearby young family with their home and buy some of the materials because they could not afford them. When the family thanked him for his generosity he told them the story of the broken down car and the incident that caused him not to pay the young man back. He said the generosity of the money was from the young man and to give a little prayer of thanks for that young man and a hope and prayer that the money that young man lost would be made up somehow.

What happened to each of the individuals? What was each person's response to the situation? Why didn't other people stop to help the person with the broken-down car? Was the wife wrong to be upset at her husband? Were there any better or worse ways to think about what happened? People respond to situations differently based on their perspective of the facts.

"Perspective is everything." This comment has been attributed to philosophical thought; famous poets and writers have commented on it often. Perspectives can also be different for those experiencing the same event. Each individual involved will have a different viewpoint from the other and neither truly objective. Whether we look at perspective as something taught or a part of the experience of life, perspective controls our actions and reactions.

Perspective is often thought of a way of seeing and relating to the world around us. It is the lens through which we choose to observe, gather information, and come to conclusions as to the action that has occurred. Think about it this way. You wake up in the morning, you go out for a cup of coffee, and the person in front of you decides to pay for your cup of coffee. Often you are happy and maybe even grateful for saving the cash. Later on you go to the grocery store and the person in front of you in line is short a quarter, and you give them the one in your pocket. When you drive home, someone cuts in front of you and you can tell that they were trying to make the exit. Instead of your normal reaction of cursing and getting mad, you actually seem to understand their dilemma and hope to heavens they don't get themselves or anyone killed.

Are you any different than you were yesterday? Maybe today you are in a generous mood and your perspective hasn't changed. Or has it? The lens through which you are seeing the world today is slightly nicer due to someone's generosity and just a general good day. You made a decision somewhere in the morning to make it a good day, and even the person who cut you off won't ruin it. Sometimes we feel so hard wired toward negativity that no matter how our day started we will seem to have a bad day. Conversely, some people seem so hard wired to be happy that they will make sure it is a good day. Perhaps it is just brain chemistry that controls our perspective or simply the sum of our experiences that has taught us that life is hard or easy, but maybe, just maybe, we do hold the key to our own happiness. Seeking peace and treasuring joy is very much something that helps us to live very happy lives. Peace begets peace, and joy shared will propagate joy. We can choose to make differences in the way we think and the way we act, though I would be the last to say this is an easy task. It isn't easy to remember when the people around you have learned how to infuriate you so.

Would we be living a lie to say that the person who cut us off on the road may have not seen us or was distracted? Why do some of us insist they meant to cut us off, potentially kill us? As if that total stranger's real motivation was to aggravate your high blood pressure. Okay yes, being cut off is dangerous, and luckily we survived. Experience the moment and then move on with your day. If you find yourself retelling the story over and over throughout the day, this reaction is not a healthy one. Don't let the "baggage of life," those times and memories that we seem to carry with us, control who you are now. Whether that piece of baggage is a day old or years old, don't give it the power to control your life for tomorrow or even years to come.

The pressures to get into college

College Plans

Often those in high school who have plans for college with the support and fervor of their parents feel a level of pressure to get into the right school or getting the scholarship so the dream of going to college and becoming a college graduate can be attained. They feel so much pressure in fact that when they fail on a test, project, or even class, they feel as though they have failed themselves, failed their families, and have ruined their life. This level of pressure does not help either adult or child. Parents become stressed and find themselves yelling or raising their voice, and the idea of failure becomes bigger than the reality of life. Sometimes the idea of this gloom is so large it supersedes the want to continue on with life, and suicide becomes an option to a person who otherwise would never have thought of this as an option at all.

This is when perceived reality and objective reality are completely different. The fact is, even if a person failed half their classes, they could still attend college. Maybe not the college they wanted, or maybe they have to go another route. By attending another college and doing well for a while, they could eventually transfer into the college they wanted in the first place. Failure on a test or even high school course is not the difference between life and death, yet many young people do not see that. Some parents do not either.

A perspective of understanding

Create a perspective of understanding. Do not make excuses for others but realize that they may not be "out to get you." Often our own paranoia creates a dimension to our day that does not afford us the ability to escape our own mental prisons, which then become our own source of turmoil. If your life has been full of people letting you down and their poor decisions have hurt you, trying to be understanding is more difficult. But trying to understand where people are coming from will only increase your ability to express patience. In so doing, we develop the fertile ground for increased peace, joy, and overall lifelong happiness.

Moments of stupid

We all have experienced moments of stupid. These are the moments where we make snap decisions that are illogical or void of common sense. These are the moments where we say to ourselves, "What was I thinking?" If we fall into this area of "lack of thinking," give others the benefit of the doubt that they may have experienced their own stupid moment.

Think of all the accidental times people may have cut someone off on the road because they almost missed a turn or a car was in their blind spot. Driving incidents happen all the time where there are near misses, and sometimes accidents are caused from the simple fact we are human and we get distracted by objects on the side of the road or perhaps we are driving slightly more emotionally than we should. Driving when we are too angry, sad, celebratory, or just plain not in a mood to concentrate on our driving leaves open room for the moment of stupid.

Have you ever known a person who will show up to a gathering and inadvertently insult or say inappropriate words? The thing that is worse is the fact that this person making all the statements doesn't seem to have a clue that what they are saying is inappropriate, and there is no malice in their voice. This may not necessarily fall in the area of a moment of stupid, but take the situation the same way. Ignore them or better yet when no one is around, explain to them that their comments weren't taken the way they meant them and explain why. Ignorance is only bliss until the person loses their job because of it.

How about the times that someone mentions something inno-cently and all of a sudden another person becomes agitated or starts to ream into the speaker? Often half the group doesn't know what is going on. Later on you find out that the person took the innocent comment personally because they thought the speaker was address-ing them directly. Sometimes a totally innocent comment given in the wrong place, timing, and company can turn into an uninten-tional insult. It is possible to mean well and no matter the intent, someone can take an innocent comment and twist it or take it wrong. We all have difficult periods of time in our lives when we become more sensitive to comments that may have not been directed at us, yet we take a comment the wrong way. It is up to us to be as under-standing as possible. If not understanding, try to ignore comments that annoy or seem hurtful. Our lives are busy and full enough not to add another's ignorance or moment of stupid to our day.

In times of financial hardship, people tend to have moments of stupid that can be quite costly. There have been multiple periods of time in the global economy where many people have found themselves having to live more frugally. The unfortunate aspect of this is the fact that a lot of people are not able to change their spending habits accordingly. Some feel a sense that they have to outwardly live with the same spending lifestyle. Don't fall into this trap. Our want to feel accepted can get us into trouble if we choose to say yes to a night on the town when we only have a few dollars in the bank. The moment of stupid in this example is when a person knows they have a few dollars and decides to go out and increase their personal debt. It is okay to say, "This month's a little tight on cash. How about going some other time or to a more affordable place?" It is also possible to go out for drinks and conversation without spending too much. Basically make deci-sions that will help you enjoy life in the present and for the long haul. Getting into debt when you live paycheck to paycheck isn't worth it.

Basically, we all have our moments of stupid and sometimes just ignorance. Give others the benefit of the doubt that anytime they have annoyed you that it is not intentional. Possibly it is because you might be a little sensitive to comments based on what is going on in your life. Either way, give yourself the freedom to enjoy life and not let others' actions or comments negatively affect you for more than a brief moment, if at all.

Forgiveness

It's a bit cliché to say "forgive and forget," but there is something to it. Without forgiveness, peace becomes almost unattainable. Can you imagine a person saying they are able to experience joy while holding a grudge or anger for something someone did a decade ago? They could be having fun, and then a sound or sight will remind them of a bad event that they haven't forgiven people for only to make the day a little less fun or downright miserable. Forgiveness is the gateway for love, compassion, peace, and joy.

Let's face it, we all make mistakes. Some mistakes are easier than others to forgive. At times there are people who will intentionally hurt us and usually for their self gain. When someone hurts our feelings or injures us physically it may seem impossible to forgive them but it is important that we do.

So what is forgiveness? Let's start with what forgiveness is not. Forgiveness is not saying or implying to someone who has hurt another that what they did is okay. It is never okay to do something mean and intentionally hurtful. Malicious actions involve thought and individual choice and that is usually the thing that hurts the most. We are not expected to forget the lessons that we have learned from people who have hurt us. If someone hurts us, we are not expected to make them our friends nor are we to believe that what they did is all right, but we should forgive. Forgiveness is less for the people who have done us wrong and more for ourselves. We also need to forgive accidents that have harmed us or those we love. Accidents are things that happen not by choice and are often not avoidable. Maybe the accident was caused by a moment of stupid that we all could be guilty for on any given day.

Forgiveness is the letting go of the hurt and personal feel of injury that another person inflicts on us. Sometimes we go through shock, denial, and sadness and mourn the injury and/or loss, but we need to move on. It is in the stage of moving on that we are more able to forgive. When we forgive, the feeling of hurt won't turn into bitterness or become a deep-seated anger. We give up the anger and want to seek revenge and let go of the pain felt at the time of the offense. Forgiveness gives us freedom from the event or the hurt and negativity of the situation. When we forgive, we allow ourselves more control over the end result of the hurt and gain freedom in our lives. If we choose this freedom, we will also be able to forget a little easier those things that bring us sadness. It is impossible to hate a person if they have been forgiven. Hate is the antipathy of love, and therefore it is impossible to be in a state of peace and experience the most euphoric joys with hatred in one's heart or mind.

Forgetting the bad to make room for the good

The little girl

Once there was this little girl playing in her front yard with her older brother. She had taken his truck and threw it over the low chain-linked fence into the back yard, making the young boy very angry. In his anger he threw the little girl's teddy bear into the middle of the street. She knew that her mommy and daddy would be very mad if she went into the street, so she ran crying to her parents. She hoped they would get her teddy bear from the street before it got hurt.

As the little girl and parents reached the door, they observed a van of what seemed to be teenagers stopped in the middle of the road, heard the van door close, and saw the van leave. When the van left, the teddy bear was no longer there. At the sight of her teddy bear being gone, the little girl with tears streaming from her eyes ran to the front yard, checked the sidewalk, and ran to the back of the yard hoping somehow it was not her teddy bear that the van had stopped for and left with. In the back yard she saw her brother standing, looking at the road from the side of the yard. She then yelled at the brother to show her where he had hid her teddy bear while she was getting her parents. He turned toward the little girl with tears welling up in his eyes and told her that the van stopped and her teddy bear was gone.

Her little heart was broken. That teddy bear had been her friend through all the moves her family had made because her daddy was in the military. She played with the bear; when she was upset she cried and told the bear all her problems. He was with her when she fell off her bike and when the training wheels were taken off. Her teddy bear was the only thing she owned that was hers and hers alone, and now he was gone. She wanted to put up posters that she had created on paper with a drawing of her beloved teddy bear. It said "Lost tedee bar" with the scribbling of a child attempting to draw her toy, but her parents told her that it is gone and to forget about it. She mourned the loss of her teddy bear for weeks. Her parents did not understand why she was so sad at the loss of a simple toy. Her brother apologized but could not console her no matter what he tried to do. He offered to give her the truck she threw to the back of the yard. He tried to make her a bear from his old clothes by tying the pieces into the shape of the bear.

Though the sister knew he was truly sorry, she could not accept anything else other than her teddy bear.

One day, the little girl's parents pulled her aside and told her they were sorry for the loss of her teddy bear and they understood that her bear was a very special friend of hers. Maybe the people who now had her teddy bear also had a little girl who has never had a special friend like him, and maybe her bear was being loved by that little girl. The little girl in frustration said that the other little girl should have gotten her own teddy bear. The parents realizing that this tact was not going anywhere, told the little girl they knew nothing could replace her old teddy but she could always remember him.

She calmed and sulked in her parent's arms and started to sob. At this, the parents told her that they were walking in a store and saw a lonely teddy bear that needed a friend and they had bought it hoping that it would not be lonely any more. The girl slowly looked up to see placed on her lap a teddy bear very similar to the one that was taken, but this time with a red ribbon around its neck. She looked at the teddy bear and then to her parents and exclaimed happily that they had found her teddy bear's sister. She took the bear and started talking to the new teddy bear about her brother bear and how she hoped they would find him, but in the meantime he might be someone else's friend until they could be back together. That little girl never forgot her little teddy bear and the way it was taken, but her grief for the loss of a friend was lessened by the finding of her new teddy bear and friend.

Sometimes, to be able to forget the sting of a bad event you need something to take its place. The little girl's story of the teddy bear is a child's way of grieving a loss. Her memories of her lost teddy bear are still with her, but the sting of the loss waned in time and a new friend helped to comfort her into new memories and a fond beginning.

As adults, a teddy bear may not be what replaces or softens the blow of a difficult time, loss, a bad day or catastrophic event. So what can we do to lessen the pain or anguish? Do we choose to confide in a friend, vent to a family member, grieve, or do we take drugs, or drink alcohol to wallow in our self-pity, anger or despair? Do we engage in sexual actions of lust or self-indulgence in the hope that our short-term physical pleasure can drown out the memories or feelings of loss? Do we allow ourselves to feel the sting of the loss, mourn the loss, talk with a friend or confidant, start to heal, and continue on knowing one day the loss or anger won't be as strong?

Often the depths of our hurt, disappointment, or anger toward an event, person, or loss depends greatly on how much of ourselves we invested into the situation. At the loss of a car or a house, it is often not the physical loss of the objects in and of themselves that causes so much grief, but the symbolism many attach to the objects. Yes, the monetary loss is definitely a blow. With tight incomes and financial restrictions, replacing of these items can become a serious cause for concern. More often the loss of the dream home or car is a reminder of our mortality, and losing the safety and comfort that are connected to the vehicle and the home causes so much of the grief. If so much thought and investment are put into such objects, how much more of ourselves do we invest in those individuals we have let into our lives? The level of our attachments also will manifest the level of loss that we feel.

It is one thing to lose a home and another to lose a person. "Home is where the heart is" says more about where our emotions lay. This is where the investment of our time and energy is the greatest. Things that can be replaced are easier to grieve for due to the fact that they may be reproducible. No, not the original, but a replica can help with the memories and maybe improvements can be made. When there is a loss of a relationship and maybe even the individual has passed away, we are reminded that there can never be a person like that again. Each and every person is a unique and irreplaceable being. Our investment in time, emotions, and intellectual engagement are also irreplaceable, and therefore we hold the importance of these people ever so close to our emotional happiness. It is for this reason that many people are so guarded in allowing another into their emotional sphere. Previous hurt or loss tends to be hard hitting. In a self-preservation mode, some people will even sever their desire to ever have these emotional attachments again. So what do we do when we feel this hurt, loss, grief, bad memory, or a life-altering event happens?

The question is how do we forget the bad to make room for the good? The fact is we don't. We don't forget the event, and we should not even try. What we do need to do is put the event in memory and try to focus on the person or the overarching lessons learned and not the event that brought us the loss or grief. The little girl lost her teddy bear. For her, that teddy bear was greatly loved. It was her best friend and confidant. To lose the bear was to lose a part of herself. She will never forget the teddy bear for she had invested her time, thoughts, and emotions into it. The event of the loss was painful and tragic. Her grief was real and her loss hard hitting. She grieved for herself and everything that bear meant to her.

When she had a new friend to fill the role, she relived the happy memories with the new bear. She made plans with the new bear knowing she would probably not ever see her beloved bear. She had gone through loss, shock and denial, anger, grief, and acceptance of her loss and chose to move on. The pain of the loss was lessened, and she chose to remember the joy and happiness that her lost bear and the relationship had given her.

You may say that a bear isn't like losing a person. Yes, a bear could be replaced, but the little girl's reality was just as hard hitting as the loss of a person. Remember that everyone has different realities. We can all be in the same room and experience an event, and every single person in the room may have a different story for that same event. Minimizing or dismissing another's pain or loss never helps the situation.

In order to find peace and discover joy we need to be able to accept the event as an occurrence and deal with it. Deal with the loss and move on. Recalling the good memories and choosing to hold them at the forefront and most immediate part of our mind will help us as we move forward. Yes, we experienced a loss and grieving is important, but choosing to remember the positive aspects of the relationship will in itself give us a chance to appreciate memories and start to heal from the grief. Even though we know that we may not have that same experience with the person again, the memory and time spent will remain with us. Just like that little girl remembering how her teddy bear helped her with the moves to new neighborhoods, there is peace in knowing that she had done it in the past. Because of the experience, it will certainly help her with future moves and new experiences. She has moved on and will fondly think of her bear in times to come with a smile, for grief is meant to be short lived.

New and pleasant memories can't replace the loss but can soften the hurt and help the healing process. If it is a loss of a friend or family member (this includes pets), it is important to grieve, but instead of filling the grief with a heavy sense of personal loss, try to remember the good times and the feeling of being with the person. Most of the time when we grieve, we are not grieving for the person we have lost but the fact we have lost them. When a loved one dies it is the companionship and accessibility to the person that hurts the most. Sometimes our loss feels like it can consume us, and in hopes of avoiding the pain we may choose to forget. But why? When we remember the good memories of our loved one we keep them alive within us.

Maybe we just lost a relationship. No one died, but the once loved person in our life has left. We invested ourselves in that relationship and gave all we are, and that person threw it away. This relationship also needs to be grieved for. Often people halt the grieving process and stop at anger, forgetting all or most of the good memories to try to figure out where it all went wrong. Then the blame game becomes a large part of the emotional investment from this point. There was a reason for the relationship to have started and grow. Though the relationship did not continue the way a person hoped, at least there was a relationship at one time to have been happy about. The loss of relationship feels like a loss and therefore needs to go through the whole process from loss, shock, denial, anger, grief, healing, acceptance, and moving on. Try not to escape the old memories. Escaping means you are not dealing with the event, and often when we do not deal with the issue or the event we find ourselves reliving the event or trying to synthetically suppress the memory from coming up at the most inopportune times.

Remembering the good and reliving the happy memories

The store greeter

There was once a woman at a department store whose job was to greet people as they came in. Every time a person entered the door, she would smile and greet the customer with a word or two of welcome. It was common to see her speaking with people, smiling all the while. She would often laugh heartily at a customer's joke or the funny actions of a small child. One day, I asked why and how she was always able to smile and be in this constantly chipper mood. Her reply was that she had a stroke just moments after holding her new grandchild; since then her life was forever changed. From then on the only memory she could easily remember was the way she felt at that moment of happiness and pride of being a new grandmother. She had lost her ability to retain any other short-term memories and was not easily able to recall any long-term memory. For her it seemed as though the tough times of the past were forever in the past, and all she had was one happy memory to hold onto and the present moment.

Some may say that this way of life is the way to go. While reliving only a good memory and living only in the moment seems freeing, but realize she had forgotten all other happy memories. Memories are lost to her, such as her childhood, her wedding day, the birth of her children, her children's weddings, and being the mother of the bride. The lessons of life afforded by the negative memories are also nonexistent. The how- to of life and learned talents that can only be experienced, such as riding a bike, fixing the sink, or cleaning the stove, are lost to her. She does not have the memory or the skill to do these simple things easily or safely. Her happiness came from what many would consider a debilitating ailment, yet some think they would prefer this life. Be careful what you hope for.

If we live only in our good memories, we are crippled because we are no longer able to live in the present, which is a daily and momentary gift. Life is meant to be lived in a balance of intellectual, physiological, psychological, and emotional growth. What we choose to remember and recall on a daily basis is the tether to the positive. The fact that we can choose to recall positive memories will serve as a reminder that good things do happen and that negative events are short lived. Being able to remember and recall the negative memories and the lessons of the past is a tool meant to make everyday a little easier while realizing that good memories and events are still within our grasp.

Recalling the good memories during times of trials and tribulation will help remind us that "this too shall pass." Bad events or periods of time are just that—a short and brief time in our existence. Happiness will return. How often do we choose to remember good memories, even as brief and fleeting as the kindness of a stranger opening a door for us while we are carry a heavy load? How long before we forget the kindness of a stranger, the quick compliment, the smile and greeting in passing. It is too easy to remember the small ill-chosen action of another toward us. It is too easy to remember for an entire day the one who cut us off on the highway or the person who didn't hold the door for us when we were just behind them. We take these moments of rudeness far more personally than we should.

Have you chosen to remember the small good actions of others more readily than the bad? The memory of good times, kindness, and quiet times needs to be a choice made consciously so our subconscious might eventually make it an automatic choice of action, thought, and attainment. Choosing to remember the good and kind actions of others needs to become a habit. When someone is kind, thank them for the kindness if possible and remember that kindness throughout the day. On the other hand, when someone is rude or is not of assistance, let the feeling go and move on with your day. Do not give control of your happiness to a single moment of rudeness or inconsideration of another. Make memories of kindness habitual and they will be your doorway to peace and joy.

If there is a strong and happy memory that may be able to repeat itself, such as a day at the beach, in the mountains, or something as simple as a glorious morning when the sun comes up or looking out over the backyard at the sunset, try to remember all that was involved at that moment. These are the memories that you want to fill your head with in difficult times. These memories can be relived and made available to be experienced again in the setting of everyday life. An everyday single event in memory that can be relived may not be as strong as the day your child was born or the wedding to remember, but this memory cannot be torn by a death or divorce. Memories that can be remembered in everyday reality can sometimes remind us to relive them on the days of the turmoil. We can take charge of our day and enjoy that similar event, such as sitting out on the patio, going to the park, or another relaxing or happy action that can be planned for later that same day. Knowing that we can plan something we enjoy within a twenty-four hour period of a distressing event is a way to unwind and return to that "happy" moment. Hope of a better day or time can be manifested in an experience that can draw us toward peace and tranquility that otherwise cannot be imagined at the time. Living a happier moment in reality even when we can't appreciate that moment to its fullness can sometimes pull us out of our negative thoughts and emotions.

Bad things happen throughout a day. It is how we perceive the event and how we carry it with us through the day that can affect our ability to be happy. Do we choose to take care of the issue immediately and move on, or do we carry the weight of the negativity with us? Choose to move on and remember the better parts of the day. Letting the bad go and replacing it with the good can only serve to make you a generally happier person.

Simple moments, lasting memories

We are revisiting the idea of looking at the normal everyday moments to be able to create more chances to experience peace in our daily lives. These moments can come in the first few minutes when we wake up from a restful sleep and create a pattern and habit to assist us in beginning the day in a positive and peaceful way. Just like that cup of coffee that we reach for in the morning, we should be reaching for that moment of peace that we would like to reside in for the rest of the day and hopefully carry on through the rest of the week and maybe the month. Reality tells us that more often than not we will be bound to experience some form of grief, frustration, or stress in our day. The act of waking up to the alarm clock and the leaving to go to a job that we don't like doesn't help. Obviously the choices that we make or that we feel life has made for us can cause stress if we let it.

The simple moments that we are speaking of engage us in the areas of our life that we can control. We can choose to make it a more poignant place in our day as an area that causes peace, tranquility, or at least a moment of escape.

- Opening the window to the view of the sunrise.

- The smell of that morning cup of java or favorite drink.

- The running of water over our heads in the shower as a refreshing washing away of the previous days hardships to give us the sense of a new birth.

- As we leave our homes, the sense of calm as the dew sits on the leaves and blades of grass in the morning.

- The fresh air or breeze that caresses our face and sweeps over us to remind us we are alive.

- When we get to work and happen to have one of the best parking spots in the lot.

- Finishing a project and having someone truly compliment us on the work we have accomplished without us having to prod for the acknowledgement.

- A drive to a destination we are eager to get to and hitting every green light as if the light was just waiting for us to pass.

- Going home, walking in the door, and knowing nothing needs to be done but to relax.

All these moments lend themselves to creating a personal and inner peace in which we can experience a joy that allows the peace to flow in us and allow us to create a form of understanding for the people around us. It is at these times that we are more patient with others, and often we become more patient with ourselves. We have found the peace and in so doing discovered a simple joy.

Change things up/embrace change

We remember the good and try to forget the feeling of the bad memories. Now life is calm—or is it? Maybe everything is fine, but there isn't any sense of a dynamic life. Wake up, go to work, come home, watch television, then go to sleep. On weekends the weekly chores get done well or half baked, and then the week begins again. Peace? Is there nothing else?

In this book, peace and quiet are two different things. They may reside in each other but never is one the same as the other. Boredom is certainly not peaceful. Sometimes in our boredom, we become restless and aggravated. We may even wish for something, anything, to happen just to change things up. Finding peace to discover joy is active and not a passive state of mind.

The daily slump of life occurs because you let it. This is not the result of life dealing a particular hand to you. Look, if you find yourself at home watching TV every night, get out of the house! Go to a bookstore, coffee house, find your local library, go to a ball game. Changing one hour of your routine can make a big difference. Go on a date with your partner or spouse, even if it is to the local coffee shop. Try something new and different.

Bookstores house more than just books. You can look at a whole section of books on a topic you're interested in and might renew an interest in a hobby or an area of study that you have a natural curiosity for but have forgotten about over time. If you are married, see if you can bring your spouse or partner. See if they would like to look at a section of books they like. Spend some time asking them why they like the topics in the area. You may find out something you did not know or need to remember about the person you are spending your life with. When visiting the library or bookstore, you can usually find a board of local events or book reading, signings, and lectures. This one visit to a bookstore could potentially fill your calendar with interesting events and may stimulate your mind and reduce your boredom. Change is something that will always happen in life. Taking your life into your control and adding those events that will form it, will create a level of dynamism and change that may even invigorate you.

Coffee houses serve much more than drinks. For those of you who do not like coffee, try the teas they serve. Most of the time when we go to the local café or coffee house, is it to order a drink and run out the door hoping to get to a location on time? Often we are running to work or some appointment. When you can, take the time to get a drink and maybe a pastry and sit a spell. Bring a book or a pad of paper, or even better yet invite a friend, colleague, or local family member. It is in the down time that we can learn more about the immediate world around us. Speaking with another person will teach us more about the other person and often ourselves. It does not take a lot to make life a little more interesting. If you go alone, look around. Observe the people around you. Don't stare, just observe the dress, activity, and even drink. Learn more about people and the local environment. You might learn what that particular coffee house is being used for. A lot of small businesses and not so small companies are using coffee houses for informal meetings. It can also be a local gathering place for the teenagers or for dates among adults. What you learn from a short sitting at a coffee house could potentially teach you a lot about the area that you live in.

Do you know where your local library is? A lot of libraries are open until nine at night throughout the United States. Libraries have books, computers, and local community meetings.

There are usually community boards that offer information on special groups and clubs in the area, when they meet and where. There are books on tape that can provide real entertainment on those drawn-out drives to work. These books on tape and CDs have audio on subjects ranging from self-help, mystery, suspense, young adult, romance, and other genres, as well as non-fiction and information that can help you better your knowledge in your own career. Often it is your tax dollars at work, so make use of your local library. The events that the library might have in your area of interest will also provide a means to meet people who have your same interests and likes as well.

There are a lot of great pastimes. Football, basketball, base-ball, volleyball, golf, and many more sports are used as a form of entertainment and activity. Have you ever watched a game on the television and then went to that same type of game in person? Talk about a whole different experience. Some may say baseball on the television is hard to get into. Well, anyone that has gone to a baseball game in person whether professional leagues or minor leagues will tell you it seems like a whole different ball game. The energy and sound of a live game is so different in person. Even if you do not know much about the game, the crowd will tell you. Just sitting and watching the people around you at a ball game may be more entertaining than the game itself. Inviting a friend, neighbor, or colleague could up the interest level for the both of you. One person may catch something from the game the other person missed.

If you are in a relationship, go on a date. If the joy and interest has fizzled in the relationship, bring it back to life. Bring home flowers, their favorite food or a new item of interest for your part-ner. Ask them out on a date (ask, don't nag). Go to a restaurant, even a fast food restaurant will give you a chance to experience something new together. This date does not have to be expensive, just a place outside the norm and something that can provide a means of conversation. Ask those questions that you would ask of a stranger. This is especially good if you do not know the answer. Over time as we have gotten comfortable with our partners, spouses, and even friends, they may have changed a little and we have failed to notice. What is their favorite color, food, car, dessert, book, genre of movie and other likes and dislikes? If you notice some of their answers are different than you thought, ask them why they like their new topic. Enjoy the answers and changes. When was the last time you asked them what their dreams and aspirations are? You might find you have more in common, or you might want to help them meet some of these goals and dreams earlier in life. You might find yourself smiling, laughing, and finding peace, joy and maybe a better relationship for the attempt.

A life that seems like it can't move forward and does not seem to offer the opportunity for peace means something has to change. Some may say the definition of insanity is to do the same things you have always done while expecting different results. Change is good.

Chapter 4
Discovering Yourself

When we decide that we want to live a life of happiness with peace and joy as an experience we want every day, we need to be honest. We need to see who we are and take an honest look at ourselves. Who are we really? Do we have a mask on and work toward fooling ourselves and others as to our true nature and personality, or are we simply who we seem to be?

After reducing or getting rid of those things that make it very difficult to be happy, we start to shed some of the masks we often build. When we can assess our perceptions and how we deal with stress, we need to figure out who we are and who we want to be— not for others but for our own benefit and personal growth. The more we hide who we are from others, the more fearful we tend to be. If that's the case, how much more troubled are we when we try to hide our nature from ourselves? Who we are, how we think, and what we believe directly affects our happiness and the ability to find peace and discover the joy we seek in our lives.

Self-acceptance

Those people

Once there was a young man in college who excelled academically and avoided any close relationships. His relationship with his parents was guarded and marginal. He grew up in a household that valued hard work and education, finding the right person, getting married, and having children. He knew early on that he had no interest in girls, but his schoolwork and specifically science was his passion. Later on in high school he was introduced to the concept of same-sex relationships and the idea of homosexuality. He came to the conclusion that he was probably gay. His parents would talk venomously about such things, so he knew that a life of homosexuality was not a concept he could consider. So he focused ever more on his academics. He liked his studies, so that wasn't too hard. He had the normal crushes on people in high school but they would be other guys. He thought of himself as a freak of nature. When something about a political battle over homosexual issues came up in the news, his parents would make a quick comment that "those people" were going to go to hell. For all his life his parents were sure that those types of people were evil.

He did everything he could to prove he was good. He got good grades and took care of his parents whenever he was home from college. He even tried to date some of the girls in his advanced classes, but there was no real interest in them for anything but regular friendships. He could not get intimate with anyone. He found his studies more interesting, and not too many people liked to talk about cellular structure or conveyance of electrical pulses through organic materials. So he started to set himself outside of society and his classmates. He achieved academic success, but he felt ever more lonely.

One day he could not stand it anymore, feeling he was condemned to hell for who he was inside even though he knew he was doing everything else right. In the depths of depression and anxiety he attempted to end his life. Though suicide meant he was going to hell, he knew from his own parents' mouths that being gay had the same fate. Though he did nothing to make anyone think he was gay, he could not fool himself. After drinking way too much, he swallowed as many pills as he could and fell into a sad and deep sleep.

Though he would have died alone in his room on any other weekend, in his troubles he must have forgotten that his mother was scheduled to visit him just hours later. In anticipation to see her son, instead of driving the several hours, she had chosen to fly and rent a car. His mother in fact had shown up to his room just an hour after the start of his sleep. She had knocked on the door to announce her presence, but she had her own key. When he did not answer, she allowed herself in and started her normal motherly help of cleaning his apartment. When she got to his room, to her astonishment and dread, she saw him and the bottles by his bedside and immediately went to her son. He didn't move a muscle despite her best efforts to wake him, and she feared the worse. She dialed 911 with despair and helplessness as she could do nothing more but wait for them to arrive. Her mind raced for the reason why he would have done this. She rode in the ambulance with him and called her husband when the hospital staff told her she had to sit in the lobby or go home and rest. The paramedics called the incident an attempted suicide, so the police were called.

He was in critical condition throughout the night. The doctors had run blood tests that confirmed that he had overdosed on over-the-counter medicine. No other drug or sign of physical abuse was on his body. Though the doctors had gotten to the young man in time and pumped the deadly concoction out of his stomach, he lay in a state of coma. There were no letters explaining his actions, and all the parents could do was wait for their son to wake. The mother in her need to be

useful had cleaned his apartment so well that the furni-
ture gleamed and the countertop sparkled. The family
asked for prayers for their ill son. They had not told any
other family members or their prayer groups why their
son had fallen ill. When he finally woke, he refused to
speak with his parents. He started mandatory meetings
with the hospital's psychologist. On his mandatory and
continued psychological review, he was convinced that a
meeting including his parents was necessary.

In the meeting with his parents, the psychologist
instructed them to remain calm and not to respond
until after their son was done talking and the coun-
selor had given an approval for them to respond. The
son told his parents that he knew he was gay and that
he never did anything about it, and yet he felt that the
condemnation to hell by his parents had made him
feel life was not worth living. His father started to stand
and respond to his son's talking to try to stop him from
continuing. Instead the psychologist with a look of com-
mand was able to stop the father in his tracks. When
their son was done with his story, the mother and father
sat in disbelief and his mother started to cry.

The father could take no more and started yelling at the
psychologist for brainwashing his son and stared at his
son telling him to stop hurting his mother. At this, the
mother's sobs stopped and she mouthed something no
one could hear. The psychologist asked her to repeat
herself. In a shaky and sob-filled response, the mother
said she had known and that was why she had stopped
saying that all gay people go to hell. The husband had
no clue what she was talking about. The son sat staring
at her, thinking back to see if her comment were true.
He realized it was, and he even remembered her saying once that as people we don't always correctly understand what the good book says.

After that, the son went back to college with occasional psychological evaluations and stayed in contact with his mother. He no longer believed himself to be a freak or to be condemned to hell. He joined another church and has started to build friendships without the fear that if they found out he was gay they would reject him. Though he accepted his homosexuality, he continued to live a life of academic passion. He now has friends that are also gay and in total acceptance for who he is and his decision to remain scientifically focused. He delved into his research and became one of the leading scientists of his day. His father did not speak with his son for many years, but after much prodding from his wife he started to communicate with him by phone. He started to slowly accept his son, not for his sexuality but for the man he had become.

This story is a reminder that we have to accept ourselves as we are. How can others accept us if we do not accept who we are? Whether we are heterosexual, homosexual, heavyweight, thin, no matter the sex, race, gender, or size, we all are important. We often measure ourselves by the way our families, society, or media portray other people who seem similar. Why? The fact is it is easy to criticize our flaws, or what we "think" are flaws, than to celebrate our strengths. Instead, let's think of ourselves another way. We can be beautiful to ourselves. We are important because we live and have the ability to laugh and smile. We deserve to be happy. Things happen in life, but we survive time and time again through the troubles, sadness, and hardships. In all that life brings, we can catch ourselves laughing or enjoying a moment of calm. Life gives us chances to become more than we thought we could be and greater than what others have expected. Accept the you that you are. When we accept who we are, we might be surprised how many others will accept us for who we are as well.

Though we might want to change, we need to accept ourselves at every stage of who we are. When who we are and how we live our life fall into direct conflict with what we believe, then something called cognitive dissonance comes into play. Acceptance of ourselves and living the lives we feel we should is vital to living happily with who we are and who we want to become.

If we are addicted to food, sex, drugs, alcohol, or anything else and want to change who we are, first we need to accept what we are this minute. In order to make plans for changing the reality of today, we must understand our current situation. First we need to know what we want to change before we can begin to change it. Many twelve-step programs and programs for change have this as their first step. When we have decided to confront such challenges in our life, we need to recognize when we can't do it alone and need support. Get help if you have illnesses that are stopping you from being the best you can be.

Accepting who we are right now does not mean we can't, or don't want to, change. Change is possible when we have a realistic view of who we are right now. Then we can start to make plans and act on them. If we want to change our ignorance or lack of knowledge, then we plan to learn. We could read books, speak with knowledgeable people, or even go back to school. If we do not like our wardrobe, we can start to donate our clothes and acquire clothing we are happier with. Maybe we want to become healthier, but we don't know where to start. We need to know our current health and ailments, so we can focus our efforts and see the improvements along the way. The longer it is going to take to reach our goal, the more important it is to have accurate data about our starting conditions. As people in search of change generally we like to see results. Noticing the changes along the way can be fun and inspiring.

Who we are is a culmination of the physical, mental, psychological, intellectual, and that part of us that has compassion and love for others. Peace and joy reside in the calm of it all. Accepting who we are is key to finding peace or at least the first step in that direction.

"Thought"

Our thoughts control much of what we say and do. How does that affect how we look at finding peace and discovering joy? What we think, we might say. What we say, we might do. Saying or speaking of something is an action in and of itself. Therefore our actions are the manifestation of our thoughts and words. There are many religious texts that will say this in many different ways. Choosing to change the way we think will show in our actions and slowly become a habit. Our thoughts, beliefs, and reactions to the world around us have everything to do with being able to experience peace and joy more frequently.

How do people change the way they think? Well, you are doing it right now. You are taking a moment to understand how you view the world. Thinking about what affects the way you think is all part of the process of knowing who you are and what motivates you. If we tell ourselves that we are the way we are and cannot change, this becomes a self-fulfilling prophecy. We can create our reality from the limitations or objectives we set for ourselves. You can create your own freedom and peace of mind in the way you think and perceive the world. You are also free to create your own hell and turmoil. You are your own tool to acquiring calm, peace, joy and tranquility.

Self-projection

As kids, we learned from all kinds of words and pictures projected onto a screen or a wall. As we grew up, we had projects that other people graded or used to measure our success. Parents may have told us how we dress or take care of ourselves is how people will judge us. As we pass people on the sidewalk, we make judgments and assumptions. We based these as much on our experiences, biases, and prejudices as anything we actually saw. Too often, we decide in an instant what people are like, who they are, and if they are trustworthy. Just as we learn and judge by what we see, hear, smell, and touch, others will judge us as well. It is not good to judge people and places we don't know. It is human nature to make snap judgments about others; it was likely essential for our own self-preservation. How do we make all this balanced and fair? How do we project who we are to those around us?

We project who we are or at least how we think of ourselves every day. When we feel like chilling out, we dress in the most comfortable clothes we have. If our friends see us, they know what kind of mood we are in by our facial and bodily movements. When we feel like we want to look good, we will dress in what we believe looks good on us. When we want to not be noticed or just disappear in a crowd, we will dress the way we think will make us "blend in." Sometimes we announce to everyone the way we feel by the way we dress and act, while not even allowing ourselves to realize how we really feel. Whenever we are trying to pretend we are something we are not, something in how we dress and act will look a little off.

Whether we like it or not, we project who we are without realizing it. It is one thing to dress a certain way and wear our hair in a specific style. No matter what our style and dress, our actions, language, and physical movements tell a lot to the people we meet. We can let people know we are happy, sad, mad, or scared with just our facial expressions. This is a small example of how we communicate to the people around us. When we are feeling good about ourselves or proud of an accomplishment, we tend to hold our heads high and carry a smile on our face. Conversely when we are having a bad day, our body might hunch over a little with a face that is more tense or wan.

Now, imagine being really happy. Imagine feeling like the world is going your way, peace is yours, and you are having fun knowing this. Pretend this is a secret that you hold. How do you feel just thinking about this? Often what we think projects in our face, the way we stand, even the way we hold our head. In many fields of work, especially anything to do with sales, the term "fake it till you make it" is used as a way for people who may not feel very confident to at least project confidence. Another way to think of this comment is if we search for peace and joy and want happiness daily, while still dealing with the bad things that can happen on a typical or atypical day, we can still smile and take on each challenge as it comes. No matter what we are wearing, our thoughts will have much more control over our physical movements and project our mood.

Some people choose to create a façade and work diligently throughout the day acting, dressing, speaking, and treating others a particular way in hopes of fitting in. Some individuals are expected to project an image or do so for simple acceptance. Some careers, workplaces, and groups of people demand this of their employees and even patrons. If the expectations and what we try to project is not far from who we really are, then going to work with a particular façade is not too difficult to keep up. Eventually what we had worked to project may eventually be who we really are and what we feel. If we believe in the idea of the certain dress, actions, or speech, then we are well within our comfort zone. When we work or have to be in a place where we are expected to be a certain way and yet we don't believe in where or what we do, then it becomes difficult to work in those environments. Who we are becomes compromised, and animosity for what we do will start to creep in. If this is the case, then something has to give, whether it is to get another job, go to another place, or buy into the idea. Peace and joy becomes much more difficult to experience when we oppose what we do every day. Our temper and stress levels will become increasingly difficult to keep in check. Realize that putting on a façade of style or lifestyle that does not match who we are will become the cause of self-inflicted stress in our lives.

We project who we are by what we wear but more importantly by what we think about ourselves. When we are generally happy and can live a life of peace and joy, it will show. When we accept who we are and choose to have thoughts that are generally positive, we will project the feelings we have for ourselves and those around us.

Communicating with others

How we communicate to others tells as much about ourselves and what we think, as our dress and what we project. How we relate to others will show in how we speak and the attitude we have in all our relationships. Our communication with family, friends, colleagues, and strangers contains components to our lives that can enhance or diminish our experience of happiness.

How honest are we when we speak with our family? Are we guarded in what we tell them for fear of being judged? Do we worry that if we say something to one person, the whole family will hear of it? Do we feel better after speaking with our friends, family, or colleagues? What has our past taught us about opening up to the people around us? Have we felt burned when we have been honest? Are we guarded in what we say because of the past? When we send text messages and other forms of electronic messaging, do people feel we are bothering them more than communicating? We have to ask ourselves these questions and then try to understand how people respond when we speak with them.

Do friends, family, colleagues, and strangers look like they enjoy conversations with you? We need to understand how people react to our conversations with them as well. Often how people respond to us can give us a clue as to how much we value the communication with them. When we speak, do people seem to ignore us? If so, how engaged in conversation are we? Is it all small talk? Do we listen to the other person, or are we trying to multitask at the same time?

When we communicate, we need to be engaged in the conversation and pay attention to the person with whom we are speaking. If we are speaking face to face, then there needs to be eye contact and attention to the message being spoken. In today's world, with cell phones and text messaging, it is possible that there is one conversation going on when a person decides to text someone else a message not related to the in-person conversation. It is very important that we ignore the many distractions to our current conversation until after the conversation is over. Look, if we take on another conversation or start to text during a conversation, we are saying a lot to the person we are with. We inadvertently tell them they are not that important. We need to say they are important in the here and now.

There are exceptions to everything, but in general, paying attention to the person you are with should be the top priority. If you have a phone conversation going, stop what you are doing unless you have already warned the person on the other end that you are doing something else as well. This situation usually occurs when we are at work but someone wanted to make a quick call to us to tell us about something. When on the phone, stop reading or watching television. Most people are not able to honestly say that they have their full attention on the conversation if there are distractions. Communication not only requires attention but also genuine words. Say what you mean. Communication is much more listening than talking. When we talk, there should be a purpose outside of making sound. Generally we communicate with our movements, facial expressions, composure, language, and all of who we are.

Our beliefs

What do you believe in? This is intentionally an open question. Do you believe in any particular philosophy? What do you think about the world around you? What do you think about morals? What is important to you? Our beliefs and moral compass often denote what our responses to situations will be.

As children, while we are under the care of our parents, we learn a set of rules within the household that we live by. We learn how to take care of our health, such as how to brush our teeth. We learn how to clean and what can be considered clean within the home. Is putting the dirty dishes in the sink cleaning, or is it the loading of the dishwasher and running it? We learn that there are expectations of how we are to treat adults, siblings, and other people. When we are children, we are also taught those things that form our conscience—what is right and wrong, what is considered reasonable, and those things for which we would be punished. As we grow to adulthood, our experiences and observations of how other people treat each other are reconciled with the foundations we were taught in childhood, which becomes the revised version of our belief system. Most children hear that they should treat others as they want to be treated. A child's observations of parents and other adults, in particular how they treat others, will either affirm or contradict what they were taught. This is usually when children start to believe as their parents do or believe all adults are hypocrites. The actions of those around the children at an early age are the premises that form attitudes about others.

Our beliefs in a god(s), the universal balance, and general philosophy starts in our childhood home. It is often not until we are an adolescent that we begin to question our religion or faith formation. As we grow and become adolescents, we question and broaden our views and thoughts. Sometimes we may become almost religious zealots, and at other times we may deny all forms of spiritual teachings. We search for what we believe, whether the beliefs are our moral, ethical, or religious systems, and then we are guided by those beliefs. If we are cynical and choose to question everything, our actions will likewise reflect that way of thinking.

In short, no matter what we believe and how we think within the ethical and moral sphere, those thoughts guide our actions. What we think, the words we speak, and how we act toward others define who we are much better than the way we look, where we were born, or how much money we have. By the core beliefs that we were taught and/or have formed within ourselves, we can judge if our own thoughts, words, and actions are worthy.

What would your obituary say?

Often to understand who we are now, we need to have an idea about how we would like to be remembered. It is not morbid to think about how we want to be remembered when we pass away. It would be more morbid to not care about what effect we have on family, friends, and society.

Now that we have accepted who we are, know what we believe, and understand how we see ourselves, we can assess our lives. What do we want people to remember about us? If our lives reflect the way we want to be remembered at our passing, then we are happy with who we are. If we believe that our obituary would not be one we would like for the world to see, then there are things we need to work on. If you were told you had only a year to live, what would you do? Who would you spend your time with? What would you want to leave behind?

Time and time again we read or hear that no one will say at their death bed that they should have spent more time working. What would you spend your time and money on? If you can do these things now for yourself and the ones you care about, what's stopping you? It is up to us to understand what we want for and from ourselves. Start working on those items and issues you care about the most. If you find the list seems daunting, just do one item at a time.

Our lives are measured by what we believe and how we have shaped our lives. Others can't be expected to read our mind and know all the answers. Do you have friends and family who know you well enough to know what you wish for yourself in life? We need to know ourselves as well or better than the other people in our lives. What we believe and how we go about living our lives are up to us and not our family, friends, or any other person. If you want people to know what you do and how you would like to be thought of, sometimes it is a simple matter of telling them.

Discovering yourself questionnaire

This questionnaire is intended for you only. Feel free to read and answer the questions to yourself or write them down on another piece of paper. This questionnaire is intentionally printed so there would not be a lot of place to answer the questions in the book. Consider the idea that you may want to share the book with another person or later someone else may pick up the book from your bookcase and start to read it. It is better to write down your answers on other sheets of paper so you can eventually shred the sheets. The questions are personal and will end up being intimate in nature. Some questions may seem trivial, but if you don't know the answer, you may want to consider the question further. Before we can be the best we can be for ourselves and others, we need to know who we are and what we want. To find peace and discover joy every day, we need to be aware of those things in life that make us happy and experience life to its fullest. These questions do not have a right or wrong answer. Open-ended questions are intentionally open ended so you can come up with as many or as few answers for each question.

1. What names do you go by? This includes real names, nicknames, and terms of endearment.

2. What is your favorite name? Why is this your favorite name?

3. What is your favorite color?

4. What is your favorite animal?

5. What is your favorite game, sport, or activity?

6. What is your favorite movie?

7. What is your favorite television show?

8. What does your favorite outfit look like?

9. What kind of movies do you like in general?

10. What is your favorite book?

11. What is your favorite food?

12. What is your favorite dessert?

13. What is your favorite plant or flower?

14. Do you have a favorite scent (natural or manmade)?

15. What is your favorite genre of music?

16. What is your favorite song?

17. What is your favorite musical band or group?

18. Who is your favorite comedian?

19. What are your favorite kinds of shoes?

20. What is your favorite kind of jewelry/accessory?

21. Do you have a particular style, and can you describe it?

22. What is your favorite car, vehicle, or mode of transportation?

23. What is your favorite topic of conversation? Why?

24. What is your least favorite topic of conversation? Why?

25. What do you like to do during your down time?

26. Where do you like to go when you rest at your home?

27. What do you do for a living or spend most of your days doing?

28. Do you like what you do for a living? Why or why not?

29. If you could change what you do for a living, what would you do?

30. What do you do on weekends?

31. How much time do you spend a day in quiet without being asleep?

32. Do you like a quiet room, or do you feel like you should always be doing something? Why?

33. How much time do you spend to enjoy eating breakfast, lunch or dinner?

34. Are any of your family of origin members still alive (parents and siblings)? If so, do you know what kind of people they are? If not, do you know what kind of people they were?

35. Do you speak with them regularly (at least once a month)?

36. If so, what do you usually speak about? Do you feel better after calling them? If so, great! If not, are there any topics you would enjoy engaging in conversation about?

37. Ask yourself, "How much do I know about my family? Do I know some stories of when my parents were younger?" Have you asked them what they liked to do when they were your age?

38. How well do you know your siblings? If they weren't family, could they possibly be one of your friends?

39. Do you have friends who live nearby? If not, do you have colleagues from work whom you have anything in common with outside of work?

40. Do you feel comfortable speaking with people you do not know? Why is that?

41. When do you feel at your most confident?

42. When do you feel at your most insecure?

43. What do you think are your best physical features?

44. What do you think are your least flattering physical features?

45. About what topics of discussion can you carry on a long conversation?

46. What topics of conversation would you like to avoid as much as possible? Why?

47. Does smiling come easily to you, or is it a chore to make yourself smile?

48. Do you laugh easily at a good joke, or do you think it is important to be reserved and not make much sound at humor?

49. Do you like to joke around with people? Do they laugh when you tell jokes, or do you prefer other people carry the humor for the group?

50. Do you like one-on-one conversation more than group discussion?

51. What would you like to learn more about that might help you with people?

52. What traits do you like about yourself?

53. What kind of traits should your friends have?

54. What kinds of people do you not like?

55. Describe the traits that you would like in a partner/spouse. For these questions, partner/spouse is a singularly committed long-term relationship based on friendship and love.

56. If you currently have a partner/spouse, what traits do you like about them? What traits do you have that your partner/spouse likes about you?

57. What do you have in common with your partner/spouse? What differences do you have that complement each other? If you don't have a partner/spouse, what would the other person need to be in order to complement your areas of weakness?

58. Do you know what physical touches and actions makes you feel good?

59. Does your partner/spouse know what physical touches and actions make you feel good?

60. What do you consider romantic?

61. What does your partner/spouse consider romantic?

62. Do you know what makes you mentally/intellectually happy?

63. Do you know what foods comfort you?

64. What things can happen in a day that you know would make you happy?

65. What would you like to have accomplished every week?

66. What are your goals and objectives for the upcoming year?

67. What are you goals and objectives that you would like to accomplish five years from now?

68. What are your lifelong goals? What would you like to have accomplished before you die?

69. Do you see yourself accomplishing these goals with a companion?

70. Do you have a religious belief?

71. Were you raised with this religious belief, or did you come to figure it out over time?

72. Do you feel that you are doing what you think you should be doing? If not, why not?

73. Is it important to you that your friends have similar beliefs?

74. What holidays, religious or otherwise, do you celebrate in a year?

75. What traditions have you created for celebrating these holidays?

76. Do you want (more) children? If so how many?

77. If you had children, what would your disciplinary style be?

78. What is your financial style? Do you like to earn, save, spend, and/or invest money?

79. Do you want to keep up with the latest trends? Or do you prefer to keep items until they no longer serve their purpose?

80. Do you like to recycle and conserve, or does it not matter to you?

81. What is your idea of an ideal home?

82. Do you like yard work or avoid it like the plague?

83. Do you do your own laundry or have it done for you?

84. Do you like to cook?

85. How clean do you like your house to be? White glove clean, clean looking or doesn't matter?

86. What would a "great day" look like to you?

87. Do you mind driving a distance to see or visit a place?

88. Do you consider yourself organized?

89. Do you consider yourself a naturally motivated person?

90. Do you consider yourself goal oriented or more of a "go with the flow" type of person?

91. At what age would you consider yourself old?

92. How healthy do you feel that you are?

93. Who would you call if you needed help?

94. Do you have a medical power of attorney?

95. Do people know what your wishes are if you were to become incapacitated?

96. Do you have a last will and testament?

97. What is your favorite restaurant?

98. Where is your favorite place to just sit and talk with friends?

99. Where is your dream vacation spot? What would you do when you get there?

100. If you were to paint a mural on a wall in your bedroom, what would it be?

Chapter 5
Components of
Relationships

Relationships are integral to our ability to experience peace and joy on a daily basis. None of us live in a bubble that is void of interaction with other human beings. Even if we only dealt with people over the Internet or a phone, we still have communication with other people. To live a life where we intentionally avoid other people and places would become a life of loneliness and the initiation of neuroticism and insanity. Understanding who we are is vital to being able to have successful relationships.

It takes two

When Albert Einstein came out with his Theory of Relativity, his concern was predominantly with objects in space and time. With relationships, our thoughts about others are also relative, but instead of physical masses, we are referring to people and their perception. Relationships exist in a plane of human beings communicating in order to gain something. Whether that something is a personal or professional relationship or monetary gain, we start to create or destroy relationships at the very initial contact with another person.

It only takes one other person present or on the phone or other end of the computer connection to create a relationship. We have professional, friendly, intimate relationships and relationships with the stranger we just passed on the sidewalk. How we relate to other people is all part of a communication web we choose to have or level of isolation we choose to expand. How do we communicate that we are in agreement, express our dislikes, or announce our acceptance of others? Our body language says volumes about how we want to relate to any particular person, place, or thing. If we haven't scared them off with or body language, our facial expression may convince them to open a conversation or stay away from us. If we get beyond that point, then it is our decision to speak that may spark up a conversation, or we may let the opportunity pass us by. Our words, tone of voice, and the use of language can communicate our intent much more efficiently than nonverbal communication, but understand that you may be conveying far more than the actual definitions of the words.

If we want to build a relationship beyond the cursory hello and chit chat, we will want to build a sense of belonging and acceptance. The easiest way to do this is to smile. Have you noticed it is a lot easier to meet people with a smile on their face than someone who is frowning? We feel more able to approach people with a smile because something in our childhood taught us that when people smile at us they tend to be nicer to us and therefore we feel safer. We are actually taught this soon after we are born, for mothers and other caretakers of babies often smile at a child. Adults only frown when they do not like something. So we grow up and continue modeling this way of showing people acceptance or rejection.

Relationships need a situation that includes you and another person. Going on the idea that life is all "me, myself, and I" won't lead to healthy relationships. Because it takes two to create a relationship we need to realize that we have to be actively involved without concentration only to ourselves. Our relationships include all the people we come in contact with regardless of the medium of communication.

Something in common

For relationships to grow, first there needs to be a reason to have a relationship. Whether the relationship is professional, personal or somewhere in between, there needs to be a point of contact. If we never meet or even hear of the existence of a person, then a relationship between particular people can't exist. We need to communicate in one way or another to have a relationship. It is that continued communication that creates a relationship that grows. The "something in common" that initiated the relationship is usually the same reason a strong healthy relationship will stand the test of time.

To have a professional relationship, we need to communicate and have some form of exchange. We pay for services and products, and if the professional relationship works well for the business and the consumer, the relationship continues. The better the communication, the better the business can fill the needs of the consumer, and in so doing the consumer may choose to continue utilizing the business' service and maybe broaden the relationship by providing a positive reference or advertise by way of referral.

Building a relationship with another individual in hopes of a friendship is very similar. When we meet the person, whether in-person, over the Internet or through a friend, we often want to know what they have in common with us. When we meet in person, we want to feel accepted within moments of meeting each other. Conversation usually starts with introductions and discussion of our public life. This includes questions about where we live or grew up, where we work and what we do for a living, our reaction to current events, and what we like to do for recreation. Within the first meeting, usually within a matter of minutes, we have a general feeling of whether or not we would like to continue the conversation.

Communication

Communication is imperative for relationships to start and flourish. When we meet someone new, a single communiqué does not make a relationship grow. It takes a series of meetings and communiqués to create a defined relationship. Have you ever had a friend who moved far away? If communication is not maintained, you may wonder about each other for a while, but eventually their name slips your mind and the relationship is forgotten. Just like our long-lost friendships, the ones we hold close require communication and this needs to flow in both directions. Have you ever called for customer service, left a message or two, and still didn't get a response? How did you feel as a result? One-sided communication does little to improve any relationship, and often people feel taken advantage of or, even worse, ignored. This can make the person who chooses to communicate feel alienated.

When we communicate or others communicate with us, we need to pay attention and listen. We need to listen to the person without any form of distraction. If we are talking on the phone with a person while trying to watch a television show, more than likely we cannot give our full attention to the person on the phone. If we are talking with a person and while we are speaking with them our cell phone goes off, when we answer it the person is reduced to being more of a distraction than the phone. We live in a world where technology has made it difficult to be out of contact, so it is up to us to know when and where it is reasonable to allow the distractions of technology to interfere with daily life and routine. When technological devices distract us from truly communicating and reduce our relationships to second tier in the communication sphere, maybe we are doing something wrong.

Communication is the key to reducing misunderstanding and creating positive connections between people and all the relationships in which a person can become involved. Communication takes time, attention, and a commitment to truly listen.

Investment in time

Just like communication, time is an important component in relationships. Time is the most valuable asset we can spend. We get paid at work usually for the amount of time that we spend working. Businesses pay more to individuals with expertise in certain areas in the hope of speeding processes and increasing market share. Our families can seem alien unless we have spent enough time to get to know them. As adults, it is common to know more about our chosen friends than the family members with whom we grew up. It is all a matter of time spent.

Imagine telling Michelangelo in the sixteenth century that he had only a couple weeks to paint the Sistine Chapel. The famous paintings that are still enjoyed today may have never existed. The detail and multiple scenes would have never been enjoyed. His masterpieces bring much peace and joy to those who have taken the time to look at them. Relationships also need time to be enjoyed. The details we share of our lives, likes, wants, dislikes, and times of sadness and joy build richness into our lives.

Revealing who we are

Taking the risk to engage in a relationship is often more of a calculated risk than one we lend ourselves to openly. In business we take on the risk of suppliers and servicers, but we often do so by first doing research on the company and checking consumer reports to see what their track record looks like. When it comes to individual people we meet, we do the best we can to gauge what kind of person they are.

When we start to spend more time with the person we are trying to get to know, we often share only as much information as they share with us. If a person tells us a story of their childhood, we might share a story about ours. On the other hand, the kind of story may be different in how much it reveals about us. The more personal a story or a set of information is, the less likely we are to share such information within a new relationship. Our friends who have shared many years of good times and bad may know our intimate stories, but they may have already proven their ability to hold our information in confidence. Revealing ourselves, our backgrounds, and the good and the bad things that have made us who we are is a part of personal relationships. Revealing our vulnerabilities is one of the more difficult components to relation-ships because it shows we have a real interest in the person. This is only done when trust has been built amongst people, usually over a long time. This is also why it is harder to have long-lasting relationships if you are afraid to share such information with oth-ers. It is also the part of most failed relationships, where people are more afraid of rejection. The big fear is that if we reveal one of our secrets, maybe we will have just told them the one thing they hate about people and therefore they will not like or accept us. We avoid this situation, not by holding our secrets out of sight, but by slowly learning about them and revealing information about our-selves as that trust is built. The honest communications we share are the bricks needed to build strong relationships.

Care for the needs of the other

As we reveal more of who we are in the relationship while fostering our communication, investing our time, and exploring what we have in common, we start to care more about pleasing the person with whom we are trying to build a relationship.

If an inventor used a certain manufacturer to create an inven-tion that gains in popularity and in so doing expands the business of the manufacturer, they become vested in the interests of the inventor. After years of communication and sharing trade secrets that can assist both in maximizing their success, the two become almost inseparable. The manufacturer will care if anything hap-pens to reduce business for the inventor, and the inventor would be concerned if the manufacturer can no longer get the materials needed. Codependency can be a side effect of such a relationship.

In our personal relationships much of the same thing can happen. If we have a friend in whom we have confided and who has come to understand the way we think and the way that we can react to new information and deal with the world around us, then we come to care ever more for that person. We become able to understand that person and they come to understand us. Often we won't even have to talk to them about how we are feeling because they know us so well that all they have to do is see us or hear our voice for a couple seconds. When our relationship grows to this point, then we truly care for the person. True friends are hard to find. The natural progression of such friendships includes the need to care for the individual, because often we feel as though they are a part of us. The needs, hurts, and joys of that other person become important to us. Their joy will tend to become ours, and we would not feel comfortable observing their sadness or hurt without at least trying to help.

Close relationships become close because we start to care more for the welfare of the other person. At points the care and concern of the other may sometimes supersede the care we have for ourselves. When this is reciprocated, a very stable relationship exists and it provides a very stable foundation for building a life of peace and joy.

Chapter 6
Fulfilling Relationships

To write about finding peace and discovering joy without including relationships would be a travesty. There are many books with the singular objective to discuss and explore relationships. Some books are specific to which kinds of relationships they are focusing on and can bring much more focus and depth of understanding to this subject. The objective of this section is to highlight specific topics in each different type of relationship that can increase the experience of peace and joy in one's life. Relationships encompass so much of our daily lives that we cannot ignore its effect on us.

Family

The family we grew up with is the same family that taught us the most about relationships. What we understand about creating, growing, and maintaining relationships is in large part formed in our youth. It is in this family that we learn what love is and the idea of acceptance. Also within our first family unit, we create the fears, misunderstandings, and baggage of life that we carry with us into adulthood.

If we grow up in a strong family that teaches us that love is kind and forgiving, we will believe that relationships exist with this as a norm. With a loving parental foundation that provides structure and discipline, we are raised as well-rounded individuals. Our families are expected to give us many of the tools we need to develop healthy relationships as adults. Conversely, if we grow up in family units where abuse and neglect are more the rule than the exception, we will end up having problems building healthy relationships because we have not learned how to have a safe and nurturing relationship.

For those of us who retain bad habits from growing up within a dysfunctional family, we can learn as adults to function and to shed some of those habits. We can learn that love is not selfish or abusive. A relationship void of sharing and caring is something from which we need to promptly free ourselves.

An indicator of healthy family units is seen in the concern shown for each individual. Parents show concern for children by providing structure and setting clear and age-appropriate expectations. In return, grown children care for elderly parents. When they respect their parents' freedom and wisdom while taking care of those things they can no longer do for themselves, love is ever more shared. Fear or hatred for any family member is a sign that trust and security have been compromised. It is wrong to use fear to get our way or to punish through action or neglect because of hatred or anger. Respect and fear are two very different things.

All families have a quirk or two that an outsider could question or think is wrong. A difference that to some seems quite strange could simply be a cultural difference or a reaction to some specific experience in that family's history. These differences are not necessarily abusive or harmful. Each family has different traditions and procedures for handling everyday affairs of life. If we compare our traditions with another family often they will seem different, but these differences enrich our understanding of familial and general relationships.

If there are issues unresolved from our past in regards to our mother, father, sister, brother, or another family member, the first step is to try to talk it out. This conversation does not have to be in person. If there is a fear caused by abuse, state your case but be willing to hear what the other person has to say. If there is hurt, forgive them. Not for them, but for yourself. Don't expect them to apologize or even to fully hear you out but if they do listen consider it a step forward. If they choose to remain controlling or disregard your issues, exit the conversation as nicely as possible and move on. The point is to let go of the emotional baggage and move on with life.

Our siblings tend to be the opposite of ourselves. If there are issues between siblings, try to find a way to resolve them and leave the baggage in the past. The less baggage we carry with us from past actions of others or even our own behavior, the easier it is to move on and live life more fully.

The family that we grew up with is a large part of our past. They are our connection with our ancestors, and they should be part of the support mechanism that we use to build our future. Parents who work for greater opportunity and success for their children realize the joy of seeing that gift returned to their grandchildren. But in situations where the family was highly dysfunctional, one must leave the hurt and anger behind so we can move forward with life. Forgiveness can be given even if it is not ready to be received. Because those families make terrible support mechanisms they put the child at a disadvantage in life, but they can at least provide us with a clear examples of what not to do.

Meeting the stranger

In today's technological society, we have become a people who choose to text, instant message, video conference, play online computer games, and rush through the work day relying mainly on emails, memos, and short communiqués. We have lost the ability to create and carry on conversations. Even the way people meet each other is altered by the creation of social networks, computer dating services, and speed dating. In the past, people would meet at school, work, church, and local social events. As children, we are told not to talk to strangers. As adults, the only way to meet new people is to be introduced by a friend or introduce oneself to a stranger. Today's society has decreased human contact and social structures that promoted the socialization of would be strangers. The ability to meet a complete stranger and develop simple levels of conversation is becoming a lost art.

Children still have the opportunity to meet other children at their school, but even the schools are becoming increasingly less social. Elementary schools are still in the position to assist the children in learning to work in a social environment because socialization is part of the curriculum. On the other hand, pressures on schools to be more accountable and students to earn the grades needed in order to get into college are demanding more and more time of adolescents. The ability to congregate on a social level has been reduced. For now even the children and the adolescents in today's society have to keep up with schedules that would rival some mid-level professionals. Their schedules are filled with clubs and sports that are more an activity than the ability to congregate and socialize. Regimented activities increase a skill and add another line item on the pre-college resumes of the youth.

Looking at a sea of people at a café full of individuals who are trying to increase the space between themselves and those around them has become a social norm. More people feel as though they are not able to maneuver around a group of people. The awkward feeling of not knowing what to do when spoken to has increased. In more urban areas people are even too intimidated to make eye contact out of fear. This loss of communication and personal connection directly affects the ability to create social support mechanisms.

So what are we to do as a people in an environment less open to conversation or socialization? We must make our own opportunities to meet people and forget the idea that people want to be completely separate from each other. People were never meant to remain in a bubble. When we were born into the world, we were born with caretakers to be companions and mentors. Even though there are many people who are naturally introverted or would like to reduce any contact with human beings, most people do not mind a brief meeting with others.

Start with the simple kindness of holding a door open for someone with a child, a person carrying a load, or simply someone behind you. No matter their race or gender, courtesy is always appreciated. Instead of not saying anything as you hold the door, say something. Any of the following would do:

- Hello.

- Let me get that for you.

- Have a good day.

- Isn't the weather great?

The key to learning how to speak with complete strangers comes from the fact that we are human. We like to be treated with courtesy, and we like to feel as if others know we exist. If a person is trying to hide, a little kindness won't hurt them.

When making a comment to another person, make eye contact if possible and smile. If you compliment another person, make sure that the compliment is honest and genuine.

When stuck in a waiting room or a long line at the airport, store, or amusement park, it is like a sea of people working or playing on some handheld device. Less and less are we able to escape work or at least our electronics. When the person in front or behind you in line looks at you, say something. Almost any of the words you would say opening the door for someone you can get away with while waiting in line or an office. The more comfortable we are at saying hello to strangers, the easier it is going to be when starting conversations with people in new settings.

In work environments, fewer people are engaged in communication with co-workers in the building, on the next floor, or even across the aisle. At work, there is a need to be kind, courteous, and just plain civil. Simple gestures of kindness or saying "hello" need to be a social and cultural norm. Taking it one step further and introducing yourself ("Hello, I am _____ from the _____ department") is a better way to initiate communication in the workplace. One might be surprised at how little people speak. Fears and discomfort with the unknown are in large part reasons for the reduced civility with people we are not in direct contact with on a regular basis.

Whether at work or another public location, we are not alone nor do we live in a bubble. The need to expand our abilities at simple communication with complete strangers, to initiate and carry on a conversation, is a skill and at times an art. You have to choose to initiate a conversation. A simple "hello" is all that it takes, and then you have created a greeting. In the split second of the greeting, eye contact, and a smile, we convey so much of who we are and our openness to not stay a stranger.

Making friends

Before you can make a new friend, you have to meet a stranger. The simple hello or helpful gesture is a great start, but then what? Where on earth do we meet people with whom we have something in common? The first question that should be asked is, what do you like to do? What topics do you think are fun to discuss with another person? If you know what you like doing, finding a venue to meet new people with similar interests just became easier.

If a person wants to meet other people with similar interests, where should they go? This isn't too hard to figure out. Join a group or go to a show, conference, lecture, presentation, or exhibit that is focusing on that topic. This is where the tool of the Internet is a good resource. Most groups, private and public, are utilizing the Internet to advertise their organization and events that are open to the public in the hope to increase participation.

Information of how to join the organization and its purpose will be readily available. Check their site for any meetings that may be coming up or any kind of "meet and greet." Meet and greets are usually designed for people who are contemplating joining the organization to come and check it out. Usually these meetings are a minor sell job about the group, but many people find these meetings interesting.

Once a person decides to attend or join a group or organization, a current or senior member usually welcomes the newcomers. In the event of meetings, someone will probably ask for your name and will answer your questions. When attending a meeting of organizations, it helps that most of the time the other people will be doing a majority of the talking. Now is a great time to practice skills on greeting a stranger. If you have a friend who is interested on the same subject, bring them along and introduce yourself and then your friend. Tell the current member that you are new and/ or haven't attended these events before. Usually, that person will introduce you to other people. If the person you are introducing yourself to is also new, then you will have something in common from the beginning. Being new to a particular event or organization will help to get others interested in telling you what they know of the group and how things are run. Occasionally other attendees may inform you of other events coming up that have the same or similar topic discussed. If the other person is done speaking ask a general question. Some general questions to ask people at such events are as follows:

- What got you interested in this topic?

- What do you know of groups and events similar to this in the area?

- What do you do when you're not at one of these events?

Being able to ask questions about the organization is good when speaking with those who have attended these events before. When you ask questions of another person and they attempt to give you an answer, give them your undivided attention. If you have your cell phone on (vibrate only please) and it rings/vibrates, do not answer it. If a person is going to attempt to answer a question or engage in conversation with you, do not cut them off to answer the phone. They are the ones with you at that moment. After they answer, thank them for the information and excuse yourself if you must check who called. Tell them you will return in a couple moments and that you have to check something. Be courteous. Many people are unaware of phone etiquette. When going to lectures and other events you need to be able to not answer the phone. In your outgoing message, just make a comment that you are not available to speak at the moment but will call back as soon as possible or that you're on a day off from work. If you do not have family that is depending highly on you, the voice mail should say something to the effect that you will contact them within the next twenty-four hours.

Often when we meet people that we think we might get along with, we tend to want to share information. The information we share should be more contact information versus addresses. After having a short or possibly long conversation with the people we meet, we can plan to meet at another event, a public location like a coffee house, or a restaurant or meet up with friends. The next meeting should be within a month or even better within two weeks. We often don't realize how fast time flies by, but it does. Don't let a good thing slip away.

Building relationships, whether professional, personal, and/or romantic, requires time, attention, nurturing, and maintenance. Even more attention is necessary in the beginning of the relationship. Creating a balance of time and contact can be difficult while people are trying to learn about each other. While we learn more about each other, one person may not want the other to call or to expect to meet as often as the other. The issue is balance. If a new relationship is to grow, it is usually a good idea to talk and to meet up with one another. Some people may have some fear of rejection or attachment and choose not to meet as often. This lack of contact will cause the friendship not to take hold. Time is needed to be able to gauge whether or not the initial feel of compatibility for any kind of relationship is there. If people who have just met each other are not able to carry on a conversation, then more than likely there isn't enough in common. If two people do not trust each other even marginally enough to share any information, then there isn't a reason for further communication. In this case it is fine to just see each other at the next event or future gathering. On the other hand if the conversation carries longer than the normal five minutes and there seems to be a natural connection between the individuals, then learning more about what each other likes becomes easier and a friendship is formed.

It is one thing to make friends and a whole other thing to keep them. Or is it? When we first meet someone who seems to have a lot in common with us and we don't see any obvious sign that they are going to hurt us, we work towards friendship. Friendships, just like anything else in life worth having, require work and patience. In the Girl Scouts, there is a saying and various tunes sung with the words, "Make new friends but keep the old. One is silver and the other gold." We measure our friendships and our everyday relationships based on the time, effort, and fruit of each relationship. Friendships thrive on the mutual benefit of the relationship and the give and take that is often felt. What often starts as an evenly shared relationship might tend to favor one more than the other. This often becomes awkward for one or both people after a while. If a person were to always have to go to where the other friend wanted to go the friendship effort is going to increasingly seem one-sided. It is reasonable to predict that the relationship is about to see a rough patch. Friendships need to have a sense of equality, or one person is going to feel used and/or abused.

Friendships help to make life fuller and more complete. Unlike family, we get to pick our friends. At times our friends may even feel closer than family because there isn't the baggage of our youth or the expectation of unconditional love. With friendships there are conditions that may not be spelled out but implied. When a friendship starts to be closer to unconditional, then the words we use to explain the friendship become closer to a sense of being like sisters, brothers, girlfriends, boyfriends, lifelong partners, or spouse.

A single's life

Friendships are special. They remind us that life isn't all work and no play. Good friends also keep us grounded in a reality beyond just our obsessions, work, or problems. Friends help make being single bearable, if not fun. Traditional society has conditioned us to think a person grows up with their family, gets a job and spouse, has kids, and grows old. The point more or less is that our society tries to create social norms. In developed countries, the idea of the social norm has changed.

Single people have greater options for what life can look like to them. Now there are greater freedoms of lifestyle. From a person being able to choose lifestyles where relationships have moved from monogamous relationships that resulted in marriage to couples choosing to live together for indefinite periods with no intent of marriage. Others could choose to live in openly homosexual relationships, which now have some rights of marriage (a choice not available in the recent past). There is also the ability to remain single without the judgment of society that being single wasn't a choice, just a result of not being marketable. As a society we are free of having to be anything other than who and what we are.

Being single and living a life of peace and joy does not mean we are free of responsibility. Our responsibilities with family, work, and society are still there. It is when we fulfill our obligations that we are truly free. What does that mean?

If parents are still alive, there is the responsibility for at least checking in on them and making sure they are still alive and well. A call to check up on them should happen no less than once a month. These calls are done out of respect for the fact they raised you, good, bad, or ugly. If there are any injuries that need to be resolved, these calls could be a way to resolve differences or at least resolve not to agree. Ask how they are doing. Try never to hang up in anger. You never know if you will have the chance to make up later. Try not to ever have a reason to live with regret. People who have good relationships with their parents won't understand why this section was added to this book. The fact is too many people do not have the good and positive relationships with parents that they think they should have, for one reason or another. The fact is, parents count whether or not we would like to count them out.

At work our responsibilities lay in doing our jobs to the best of our ability and choosing to grow in competency and quality of work. Being able to rise to the occasional challenge in the work arena can be a cause for peace and joy. If we do well regardless of how others treat us, we can have peace in knowing we did a good job. We often respond to the reactions of those around us positively or negatively. If we work to prove to ourselves our own abilities, then it is almost impossible for people to control our lives at work. We have the responsibility to appreciate our own work and abilities. We have to be the best we can be, not for others but for ourselves. If we seek ways to improve ourselves and the quality of work, our work ethic will be recognized whether formally or informally. Hard work and perseverance is hard to ignore.

Society also has its demands, and our responsibilities in society mean being a good citizen. What does that mean? If something in society bugs a person, complaining does not do much to fix the situation. Be part of the solution. We are more peaceful and happy when we feel like we can do something about the problems we are up against. Instead of just complaining to yourself about the issues and problems of society, choose to do something to change it. Tell the "powers that be" what the problems are. Offer possible solutions. If you don't like the politicians in office, make sure you vote or even volunteer for the candidate you want to win. Be active in society. Look for community and charity events that are open to the public. Any time you volunteer to help other people, you are interacting with others in a healthy way and you are improving your community. Our activity will create the possibility to change the world around us, and we can smile knowing that we make a difference, no matter how small it may seem.

Being single can be joyful if we allow ourselves to take the opportunities that are given to us. With freedom from other responsibilities, a single person is free to charge full force into their family, work, and civil responsibilities, improving the world for themselves and everyone else and in so doing improving our relationships and increasing our opportunities for joy.

Family and me time

Whether we are single, married, committed to another person, living in our own home or still with our parents, it is important to remember time is needed for the family as well as time for ourselves. All relationships need time and attention to flourish. The same is true in order to understand ourselves and assess our own way of relating with people and the world.

It is too easy to say that we are too busy to spend time with another. The demands of work can seem all encompassing. Too often we work late hours or weekends trying to make sure to make ends meet. We try to live a lifestyle that meets or exceeds our own experiences that we had when we lived with our parents. While we work hard, we may like to play hard as well. At the same time we may not have the balance we need to maintain the relationships we have or the ones we are attempting to build. So how do we find balance with our personal time and our shared time?

We need to schedule time. Yes, we need to add one more thing to our list. This "thing" is called time. People who work hard to become upwardly mobile or to remain in a position of power within their field of work tend to prioritize work over all else. This could be a problem if it eliminates all time for ourselves or others. If an executive, or any other person in an organization, has a spouse and children, it is imperative for them to schedule time with thier family every week. Often, our secretaries seem to control our time; the fact of the matter is we do. If we tell our secretary to block off a period of time every week and label it "important [family] business meeting," then our associates would know that we will not be available. Often executive schedules are posted in house so colleagues can expect their absence and know to report problems to another manager. Scheduling even a small amount of time without expectation of attendance to any meeting or phone conference gives us the "me time" we need to gather our thoughts. This time can also be dedicated to the building of one's family, friendships, and other relationships. If we work in retail and work on evenings and weekends, it is even more important to make allowances during the week to spend time with our friends, partner/spouse, and family members. Money, income, and security are important, but without allowing ourselves time to foster our relationships, that security and freedom will start crashing down. We say we work hard so we can play hard, but without a person to share it with, playing hard or even existing can become a lonely place to be.

Realize time is the most valuable asset we have. We need to spend it with what we deem the most valuable people in our lives. Schedule time for relationships and keep it a priority.

The family we choose

We are born into our biological families, but as we get older we begin to have friendships outside of our family. If we are lucky, those friendships become close and we choose to adopt our friends as a brother or sister we didn't have. Maybe our best friend may end up being our lifelong friend, partner, and spouse.

As our friendships become stronger and more intimate, there may come a point where the conditions that are set in friendships become unconditional. The relationship becomes rooted in love and caring for the individual. Having these kinds of relationships are freeing because they allow us to be who we are without pretense or fear of intentionally inflicted hurt. We had time to grow the relationship, creating a caring, loving, and nurturing bond with another person.

The family we choose are those relationships that we have grown close to over time, with commitment and a lot of communication. These are the people on whom we have spent much of our time and resources. We have shared with them our wants, dreams, fears, guilt, and the pleasures of our lives. When we have relationships like this, it becomes important that we maintain these relationships with the same fervor and attention that it took to grow the relationship. As in all things, if we stop providing the nourishment needed, the friendship could wither and die. When we hear the term "growing apart," often it is more likely the relationship is not being maintained. Usually communication breakdowns have occurred and an increase of misunderstanding between people grow into chasms that can no longer be bridged.

This is true for friendships, partners, spouses, and lovers. When communication decreases or worse ceases, it is impossible for the people involved to know the changes that are occurring in the other individual's life. If a friend gets a promotion at work and doesn't tell us, then we feel hurt that they did not think of us to share such joyous information. Let's say that same friend gets the promotion and calls us, but we don't answer our phone or call back later to find out what they had to say. Then we become the one who chose to ignore the friend and therefore the relationship. Communication of our wants and desires is as important as listening and paying attention to the wants and desires of our friends.

In cases of our partner or spouse, the one where there is a singularly committed long-term relationship based on friendship and love, communication (verbal, mental, intellectual, physical, and sexual) are all important aspects to continuing the relationship. When we are in such committed relationships, our partners become a part of us. We hear descriptions of these relationships referring to the other as "our better half," or the "love of my life." The peace and joy of having such relationships are celebrated in weddings and symbols of fidelity such as the wearing of wedding rings or bands of marriage. It is for these reasons we choose to share publicly the love between people. Most couples, whether heterosexual or homosexual, want the right to publicly celebrate the intense love that two people can have. Public ceremonies of marriage are proof of the lifelong commitment to each other. This is why the divorce or breakup of such relationships affects the individuals and all those who love them. It is also because of this that it is so important that love and fidelity continue throughout the relationship, and communication on all levels is imperative.

The family we choose, whether it is that best friend that is like a sister or brother or the committed lifelong relationship, love and fidelity needs to be nurtured. It took time, effort, communication, and emotional attachment to get to this point of the relationship. It takes the same amount of work to maintain it.

The nuclear family

When we choose to have a lifelong and committed relationship we may also choose to have a family. Socially the most common family structure consists of two parents having two children and possibly the family pet. Small families such as these struggle to give fair time to each other while trying not to crowd its members. Children vie for parental attention, and parents have a balancing act between work, the spousal relationship, and providing the direction and care to each of the children as equally as possible, lest the children accuse them of favoritism. The dynamic within this family structure can be intense.

Maintaining relationships becomes a challenge, but one definitely worth undertaking. The parents may find that they have to continue to learn strategies and techniques in raising the children upon which both can agree. All families have their own structure. Often when two people decide to start a family and include children, the most common area of disagreement tends to be in the style of childrearing. Before starting a family is the most optimal time to discuss how a couple may choose to raise children. No matter the time and effort put into planning of how to raise children, its execution may change when the children arrive. We can prepare all we want, but when that child is in your arms or in your care, the world seems to change. So parents, try to be patient with one another and come to consensus. Each parent even with consensus may execute the plans on discipline differently. Try to realize that both styles are good as long as the rules are consistent. A combination of both styles may be the best for your family. Open discussion between parents is important to the peace, joy, and overall harmony in the family. While childrearing is incredibly important to discuss and come to terms with, in the end it is the strength of their partnership that will determine their success.

Parents will need to create support mechanisms to help in raising children. It is said, "It takes a village to raise a child." Well, find a way to create that village. The combination of trustworthy adults, grandparents, aunts, uncles, and friends can provide the support that a family needs. These support structures provide a means of feedback and support. This is also a good pool of people to draw periodic caretakers for the children, when parents need time alone to strengthen their partnership.

As parents, we like to control the safety and play of the children. In the attempt to control the child's environment, it is too easy to forget that we have to nurture the relationship between ourselves and our spouses. Sometimes a parent may go to the extreme of childrearing to the exclusion of care for the other parent. This is a common but often relationally fatal mistake. Parents, take time to be romantic with each other. Go on dates and talk about dreams. Don't stop talking! No person is better than another, and there was a reason for the deep relationship that you share. Remind each other as often as possible of the reason the bond began.

Smaller families may seem simple but the dynamics can be intense and at times difficult. Communication between spouses and time spent with children are the gifts that make these relationships rich and prosperous.

Larger families

With the popularity of reality television shows, many people have a skewed understanding of family. Ever more so are the distortions of understanding the dynamics and the needs of large families. For purposes of this book we will consider a large family as a unit of people that includes two parents and four or more children. Basically once a family gets large enough that the parents don't have enough hands to hold a hand from each of their children, then the family is larger than what is assumed to be easily controlled.

With large families, the support structures mentioned in the nuclear family become even more vital. All parents need time to go on dates with each other and have time to communicate, but the dynamics of the children can become more challenging for anyone they ask to babysit. One parent can't possibly go to each teacher during back to school night, and that is if all the kids are in the same school. In a small or large family, there are no two children alike. Identifying and meeting the needs of the children become ever more time consuming with each addition. It is the dynamic of these differences under one roof that make each day as much fun as it is challenging. ·

Parents in these circumstances need to learn each individual child and their needs and wants. While doing as much as possible as a family, each individual child needs one-on-one time with Mom and Dad. Time management and organization becomes a need and one that will focus on shared schedules and the attempt of the family unit to work as a team. While this may seem like a lot of work, and it is, the amount of joy that can come from a loving family can be so enormous that all the effort is well worth it.

With more children comes more work, more need to cooperate, and more support for each other. Large families provide built-in friendships amongst the children. Because no parent could pick up all the toys, dirty clothes, and used dishes of all those children, often each child is given more responsibility earlier on in life so that the family can run smoothly. Children in these situations where time and effort, love and nurture are involved tend to be responsible and caring individuals. The problems that children in large families complain about is not having enough alone time. Understandably this is a difficult issue to resolve when most houses are not built for large families. As long as communication among the children and parents is maintained and each child feels listened to and responded to, life can seem a little easier even with the challenges a large family can face.

Peace and joy in families is possible, though there will be the days where the children argue and the home is in disarray while parents try to get children under control and act more civilly to one another. Kids will argue and fight, and while they do so, parents try to teach children different ways to communicate. Time, attention, and communication are important. In all the communication, the children need to know that they are loved.

Extended relationships

"Extended relationships" refers to relatives and friends of our immediate family. Our aunts, uncles, friends of our friends, and our in-laws are all part of our circle. Often people find it difficult to deal with their own intimate family. The idea of working or considering the extended family and relationship becomes more of a hassle than most people believe it is worth.

It is the connectivity of people to each other and our surroundings that can help to expand our minds and our ability to see relationships as ever more important. Consider your extended relationships as a means to meeting strangers and possibly making a friend. Sometimes we can find the people we can relate to the most in the extended family units. It is not uncommon for a child of one family to be very similar to a related aunt or uncle. Parents may sometimes remark how a child is so much like a brother or sister of theirs or even one of the child's grandparents.

Connecting even in a small way with our extended family can be very beneficial to understanding family origin and maybe a little more about ourselves.

Relational Issues

Criticism versus truth, venting versus projecting, supporting versus enabling, growing together versus growing apart, and dealing with it all can seem daunting and the reason not to try. No matter the relationship, there are going to be disagreements and times of trouble. With those we care about, criticism for the sake of criticism should be rare. Constructive criticism helps us to grow but needs to be couched in love and understanding.

Sometimes we want and need to be the cheerleader in our relationships. This is a great way to be that support for a person we care about. The only time this support becomes counterproductive is when we become the enablers for their demise. When a child in school is caught bullying another child, blaming the other child for getting yours in trouble teaches the bully that the actions can be blamed on the other. Instead of supporting the child by minimizing the situation, correction of the child could help reduce further poor choices. If an adult chooses to shop constantly to the point of financial hardship and the best friend of that individual knows of the situation but continues to invite the friend out shopping, then the friend is enabling poor conduct and choices and not acting like much of a friend.

Our relationships with people can enhance or reduce our experience of peace, joy, and overall happiness. To take on the responsibilities and work in order to maintain relationships with our family, friends, acquaintances, and colleagues can afford us the opportunities to grow in respect and love. Treating all those we meet with respect and civility provides a means to possibly meeting a new friend. To make a friend, we must meet a stranger. In order to make a friend and grow the relationship, it requires our time, attention, and effort in communication. Families provide a means for love, support, and guidance. Given the time, attention, love, and support, families, their children, spouses, extended families, and friends have a means to always feel loved, needed, and never alone.

Chapter 7
Peace, Joy, and Society

Finding peace and discovering joy in everyday life is not just about ourselves but also how we affect those around us. If our perceptions of life change, then the way we treat others and present ourselves change as well. Being able to forgive others and trying to create peace and joy in all our relationships spill over to society. Each person affects everyone around them. A person who smiles and shares it with the next person can improve the other person's outlook and perspective, even if momentarily. How we affect others in our lives everyday can be the means to peace and joy for ourselves and others.

Peace and joy have to be shared

When we experience personal peace and a joy that almost overcomes us, we have a great urge to share the feeling with others. How often can new parents hold their joy of the birth of their child to themselves? It is normal to want to share their good news with everyone they meet. The urge to share peace and joy becomes a necessity. Even our beating heart reacts with the exuberant happiness we experience in this thing called joy. When we are closer to being in a state of extreme joy, how often do we want to jump up or holler and share with the world that which has made us so happy? The day a child is born, the newly engaged couple, newlyweds, the underdog political candidate that wins the election—all these people have felt a larger joy that often can't be easily explained. Have you ever been so happy that you felt that if you were any happier you might faint or pass out because life seems so great for that moment? It's so joyful that you are almost delirious with happiness, and the last thing you want is for someone to end that joyful buzz.

To not share the joy, peace, and overall happiness that occur in our lives would feel like a slow death. Have you ever had a piece of good news that you really wanted to share with the world but you had to wait until you told your mom, dad, spouse, friend, or relative before you could tell anyone else? How did that make you feel? Most people feel like they might pop if they don't get to tell anyone soon.

The promotion

Once there was a man who was promoted to an executive position within his company. The moment he found out he wanted to jump up for joy, but instead had to remain calm. As soon as that same newly informed executive could take a break, he quickly went to his vehicle and pumped his hands into the air with triumphant vigor. He called his wife and made a few more happy exclamations in the car, composed himself, and preceded back to the building poised and in control. He had to share his joy with the person he loved. His wife also shared in his joy. Soon after she got off the phone with her husband, she proceeded to call the rest of her family, friends and then his side of the family. Joy couldn't be contained.

We have mentioned some pretty extreme stories of happiness. How about just simply having a normal day? If a person can honestly say that they are generally happy, then the ability to help others around them experience peace, joy, or at least everyday happiness is a lot easier. We all have needs and responsibilities and have people in our lives that for some reason always try to ruin a good day, and yet we can still say we are generally happy. Happy people are allowed to vent and have sad or upsetting moments and take those needed timeouts to quickly calm down. This person may need to listen to others who can provide a sounding board to help them see the situation with a different perspective or possibly help with suggestions and solutions. This ability to understand and give feedback in order to help is the act of sharing peace and joy with others. We have all had times where we have been angry, hurt, or upset, and someone else talked us down and possibly made us feel better. The reason the other person was able to improve our mood was due to their calmer, mental and emotional state.

Peace and joy can be tangible for others when we allow ourselves to experience it in our lives and share it with those around us. How we choose to use the freedom and peace in our lives is entirely up to us. We can choose to stay at home and forget others. We can choose to tell ourselves that society and those around us need to find their own way to peace and joy and hold our gifts and abilities to ourselves. Where is the fun in that? Amusement parks are fun but not as much fun as when someone else is with us. No matter what our decision, it is rare when a person who truly is peaceful and generally happy decides not to share it with others.

What difference does it make?

The more a person and the citizens of any society can find peace and joy in their lives, the more they make a difference in the life of all those around them. Not only is the person able to handle the changes and turmoil that life may present them but they will be calmer and the stressors found in life may not affect them as negatively. Stress is the cause for many of the ailments in society today. Coping mechanisms for stress can include eating too much, leading to obesity, bulimia, and poor cardiovascular health. A plethora of illnesses can be linked with stress and the body's physiological response to stressors. The way people treat each other will also affect the support systems that make sure people are adequately housed, fed, and cared for.

It has been said that each person touches the lives of ten thousand people. Just think of how many people you can affect in a single day. When a person wakes up and leaves for work, actions on the road may predicate another person's start of a new day. If someone gets cut off on the road, that someone may complain or even worse end up in an accident in the attempt to avoid collision. When someone opens a door for a person entering a building, that act of kindness does affect the other person's initial response to the work day. Have you ever been in a hurry and while carrying a stack of papers, folders or a box, something falls to the floor and someone else picks up the item and hands it to you so you do not have to set the whole stack down? This little bit of kindness puts us in a better frame of mind. When one person is kind to another and the kindness continues from one person to the next, then the effect of a single act of kindness can catch on and carry on to a multitude of people in one day. We have all heard the stories on television or the radio how people have shared kindness and then the next person tries to pass it on. Imagine if everyone could do this every day. We would perceive our neighbors differently, and we too would change, a little at a time, the paradigms of society and life.

Have you ever spoken with a patron or cashier in a store that treated you unkindly or less than human? How did you feel about the store or the person? Could you understand their actions, or did it just infuriate you and make you think twice about going into that store again? It is often said that a store or a person who gives good service is less talked about than the person or service that has done a poor job. It is so much easier to remember the bad. As mentioned before, if you talk about the good that people do and compliment those who have done well by you or who have exhibited good behavior, actions, or something else positive, you will have made someone happier even if it is for a brief moment.

Smiles wanted

There was this story a church leader shared at a service, one of those stories that many people use with slight changes. It sounds something like this. There was this young teenager who was having a rough patch in life. She fell into a depression and a sense that she had become inconsequential, that she wasn't important to anyone and that she had nothing to add to the world. One day she decided that life was just too unbearable. All she wanted was a smile. She wanted to feel as though she mattered. She decided that if she could go through a whole day without a single person smiling at her then she was going to end her life that night. She needed to feel like someone thought she was worth a smile. She went through school; not even a teacher smiled at her. She went to the mall and visited her favorite store, and the sales clerk didn't even smile at her. She went home and could not get even five minutes of conversation. Later that evening she wrote a letter explaining that all she wanted was a simple smile. She felt that people didn't consider her worthy of a smile. When her family found her lifeless body the next day with the letter, they shared this story with their pastor, friends, and family with hopes that another child would not share this same end. This story was shared. Many people who heard this story decided to smile in the presence of other people in hopes that they could maybe be that one person who saves a life with just a smile.

Though this story may or may not be true, we can all imagine a person or event where a simple smile can make such a difference. Since it takes more muscles to frown than to smile, why don't we smile more often? Smiling often makes its wearer happier as well.

Think of those times where a simple courtesy and a smile helped to make your day a little lighter and maybe a bit better than it started. If a person is able to experience peace and in so doing discover joy in their daily lives, then the feeling of depression and anxiety cannot take a permanent hold.

Furthermore if people are able to experience a little happiness in their daily lives, then it is easier for that same person not to fall into despair. When in the midst of situations that would normally create sadness and disappointment, our knowledge that "this too shall pass" will help us through.

Everyday sayings with a meaning

In order to teach children lessons and create a common understanding of what is acceptable in society, certain sayings have been created with some success of their catching on. Just as kindness begets kindness, it is not too hard to imagine that mean actions create ill feeling towards the person being mean. "What goes around, comes around." People would refer to this as "karma." The idea that one's actions, whether good or bad, will come back to a person is a part of many different philosophical and religious beliefs. They teach that each person should be good and "do unto others as you would have them do to you." This saying is also known as the Golden Rule. Though the saying itself is often attributed to a particular set of beliefs, this is actually a well known and accepted rule of thumb for society to be able to run smoothly. Consider the idea that a lot of our laws are in response to the beliefs of society and the idea of justice. People do not want others to kill, steal, hurt, or treat them with disrespect, so laws have been created to help improve civility by defining it within law. If everyone worked off the same ideas and understood the same ethical and moral measures, there would be no reason for law, but this is obviously not the case.

There are many sayings and words to live by which have been used. Consider these sayings and how they can help you in your life to find peace and discover joy.

- "Stop and smell the roses."

- "Give peace a chance."

- "Many hands make light work."

- "It takes a village to raise a child."

- "A penny saved is a penny earned."

- "Live, laugh, love."

- "Unless you have something nice to say don't say anything at all."

Of course there are many other sayings that try to warn people of possible complications than can occur or ways to describe how one feels such as:

- "The early bird gets the worm."

- "Don't count your chickens before they hatch."

- "Between a rock and a hard place."

- "Up the creek without a paddle."

These sayings often create a community version of common sense. This is similar to the common knowledge that a person shouldn't walk in front of a car and locking the front door is safer than leaving it unlocked. Common sense and common phrases help the individual and society as a whole to function more smoothly. It can also be stated that common sense can assist us in avoiding those people who may want to hurt us. Usually we would choose not to approach a group of strangers hanging out on a corner wearing long bulky coats and ski masks on a warm summer day. Why? There's something just not right about the situation, and your common sense tells you to stay away. If the setting were different, maybe they are at a bus stop on a cold winter afternoon, or if we knew one of the people, then we might feel safe to approach. Knowledge is power and common sense a good ally.

Community and acceptance

It is one thing to be able to say a nice word to another person and share the ability to be kind and patient with another. When it comes to sharing peace and joy as a society, we have to be able to take a larger sense of responsibility for each other. This would include the ability to know ourselves and deal with the idea that other people are not like us. Accepting the person that you may call family, neighbor, colleague, or stranger is a part of creating a situation of peace and joy in the communities and societies in which we live.

What does it mean to accept each person in society? Acceptance of each person in society does not mean we have to like them or believe in anything they believe or do. What it does mean is that the people we come into contact with each day should not fear the idea of being rejected by us. When we can accept everyone as different and unique individuals, we can work toward trying to understand each other. We need to be able to understand that the person in front of us is not far different from ourselves. Each person is trying to survive, live, and thrive, just as any other. If we can be the reason that a stranger's fears are relieved, then it increases the possibility to share peace and joy on a daily basis. We can become the catalyst for peace and joy not only in our own lives but for every single person we meet.

People can sense when they are accepted for who they are without judgment and assumptions. When we meet a person who does not hold to the same ethical and moral point of view as ours, we may choose to treat them with civility and not choose to further the relationship. The difference is giving the other person a chance to get to know who we are as we learn more about them, even if it is for a brief moment. This includes those people with whom we have to agree to disagree. Accepting people for who they are does not mean to accept the other person's decisions or actions. In every family, there is a person or two with whom the family cannot seem to agree. Yet, because the person is family, we love them and know for better or worse, they are family. If we want acceptance, then we have to be willing to accept others as well.

Finding peace and discovering joy can be found through the experience of meeting new people. It is usually our own prejudices, ignorance, and bigotry that cause our own sadness or anger toward people we know little about. If we can choose to shed our prejudices even if but a little at a time, we will feel freer because our own preconceived notions won't limit us. Trying to understand why people do what they do helps us understand and appreciate our differences. We will also become less fearful of the people we may have once been prejudiced against. It is fear of the unknown and what we do not understand that usually leads to our continued ignorance and bigotry. Making a decision based on fear doesn't usually result in positive outcomes, just predictable ones. Choosing a couple people of any group to represent the whole is also a poor decision. Find peace in the freedom from ignorance and prejudice, and those around you will as well.

As a free society, we are more able to make choices that exclude and omit people from our circle of friends and daily acquaintances. Choosing to do so because of prejudice or negative generalizations does no good for us or others. This practice is the antipathy of social acceptance and mires the whole society in animosity and loathing. Accepting people for who they are gives us a chance of friendship and a freedom from self-inflicted loneliness.

The social outcast

In many communities there is an expectation for residents of the area to be a certain way. An expectation of clothing design, home landscape, and vehicle may all be a part of this. Individuality and uniqueness in many ways is not accepted in the society, and often the scrutiny can be unbearable for those who feel a need to have acceptance from those around them. If these social standards are not met, then the person who has not conformed to the social requirements becomes an outcast. This constant scrutiny and judgment can become very problematic, especially those for whom social acceptance is important. The children of the family are often made to be the outcast within this kind of environment as well.

Life becomes a little less free until the people who "do not fit in" realize that the only way to take back their freedom is to understand that they are free from those who impose their beliefs, thoughts, and expectations on others. They only have as much control over us as we give them. It is normal for people to want others to be more like themselves. People like to understand what to expect and have others know what is expected of them. It takes a person who has a strong resolve and who is secure in themselves to make the decision to not conform to the pressures of peers. The fact is, everyone is different. All people should be accepted because of their humanity, which is more important than the judgments of any man, woman, or child.

Creating the social outcast has become a socially acceptable way of bullying. To create peace, joy, and overall happiness in our personal lives, we have to make sure we are not part of this social problem. Although we can try to be part of the solution, we cannot affirm those who continue to name people as the social outcast. Acceptance of each person is the direction to work toward. This is where the saying, "If you don't have something nice to say, don't say anything at all," is most appropriate.

The bully

There once was a college student living in the dorms. She had worked hard in school and was the first in her family to attend college and did so on a full scholarship. It was her sophomore year, and she excelled in her studies. As usual she had the mandatory roommate who seemed okay but was a little too much of a partier. She didn't mind since she spent most of her days in class or studying in the library. They had little in common and ended up not talking much. When she would come back to the dorm room, her roommate would often leave and go talk with friends down the hall.

On Friday nights when the roommate was out partying, she used the opportunity to call home and talk to her baby sister who was still in elementary school. Her sister loved the children's cable channels, so she would turn on the same channel in the dorm room. It was such a joy to share these happy moments with her sister that she would begin singing and dancing right along with the kiddy shows while they were on the phone.

Little to her knowledge, her roommate had set her laptop webcam to broadcast a live video feed online. All of the immature singing, dancing, and cartoon watching streamed over the Internet for her roommate's friends to see down the hall. They had such a laugh that they decided to post the video online for everyone to see as well. By word of mouth, this embarrassing video was shared and viewed by a large portion of the student body of the college.

In less than a week the scholarship student started getting rude comments about her dancing skills and choice of music. She ignored the first few people, thinking they had her confused with someone else. But then pictures of her dancing in her sleeping clothes started showing up on bulletin boards across campus. She tried to give the simple explanation about talking on the phone with her sister, but no one was interested. The images were so amusing, and everyone seemed to be having too much fun laughing at her. She was picked on increasingly and was horrified by the attention. It seemed as though no one would let up, and her grades plummeted. She was no longer comfortable studying on campus or even being in her own dorm room. Too afraid to ask for help, she wasn't able to get her grades back up by the end of the semester. Considering her lousy grades, the college took away her scholarship and she had no will to fight the decision. Without the financial assistance she was not able to finish her education. She went home embarrassed and ashamed. Her family were simple people, who did not believe in suing others. Their daughter would eventually graduate from another college, but with debt and a severe loss of self-confidence.

Some may think this story is not very extreme but the results are still troubling. There are several severe cases of bullying that has caused the death of the victim, whether by manslaughter in a prank gone wrong or the suicide of the victim for their despair of not being able to escape their torment. It is not the victim who chooses to become the social outcast. It is the people who have branded them the outcast that are the perpetrators and who themselves are the insecure ones.

It is up to those who know the difference to not affirm excluding behavior. Every environment has its share of bullies. Unfortunately there seems to be an equal opportunity for bullying—those who would pick on, exclude, torture, or assault others in order to build themselves up. Bullies often are not at peace or happy with their own lives. No matter the mask and façade they wear, actions speak louder than any rationalization they can provide. Accepting all people for who they are and refusing to continue the exclusionary efforts of those who would count people out can create peace in our lives by creating more social harmony.

Each individual in society makes a difference, for better or worse, to those around them. People who are generally happy or are able to take the challenges of life as they come tend to be more secure in themselves and treat others with respect and dignity. Our own ability to find peace in our individual lives, know happiness, and discover joy affects society directly, one person at a time.

Chapter 8
Being at Peace

Finding peace and discovering joy is a process that can lead a person to living life happier every day and feeling more fulfilled. The peace brought about by knowing all is going to be well with you in this world, no matter what may be going on, calms the mind, opens the heart, attracting happiness and joy. Joy is sometimes called happiness, but for others joy is the combination of peace and happiness, a happiness that resides with the person longer than just a moment. Once we can remove the obstacles in the way of our ability to experience peace and discover joy in our daily lives, then we work toward a life open to experiencing happiness daily. When we treat others the way we would like to be treated, we become more able to identify ways of experiencing the joyful world around us. While working to improve our relationships, we become more open to longer lasting friendships. Once we have a life that is in a state of peace and joy, we begin to transition to sharing it with others. At this point we begin to live a life in peace. To enrich our lives, we start to grow in hope, reassess our beliefs, incorporate more laughter, grow in humility, and love more openly.

To live a life that is generally happy and peaceful requires many things working together in harmony. We need to make sure that we are taking care of ourselves physically with enough sleep and exercise, all while eating right to keep or bodies healthy. Learning something new and going with the flow will help to keep our minds alert and react to change with less stress and the ability to take on new challenges along the way.

If we are trying to deal with issues from the past, we need to find a way to leave them in the past. If we need the professional help of psychiatrists or psychologists, then we need to make use of the resources that will help us to move on (so we can truly enjoy life). Getting the help you need is essential to creating a balance and finally dealing with the issue or issues holding you back from getting control of your life. When we can have our minds clear or resolve to leave the past as a memory and a means to learning life's lessons, we can work toward keeping our perspective one of positivity in our lives. Creating good memories in conjunction with a positive perspective allows us to go through a day looking for the good in the events and people that surround us.

Remember, we all make mistakes. We all have our "moments of stupid" or instances where someone's poor decision does hurt or frustrate us. Give them the benefit of the doubt that they meant you no harm, but they too are having a tough day and just made a stupid mistake. Understand and realize that people are not out to get you. Even if there are people out to get you, your response and actions are the deciding factor in whether or not they have control over your life. Let go of your fear, anger, and hurt. Stop being afraid and guilt ridden. Fear and guilt hold us back from making good decisions and being the best person we can be. Fears of loneliness, rejection, diminished social status, and other like fears often are the thoughts and feelings that hold us back from success and independence. When we act from a center of fear, we often make poor and sometimes irrational choices. It is only when we move ourselves past our fears that we are no longer controlled by them. Change is good, and whenever we move beyond the limits we place on ourselves, we grow as people and come closer to freedom from our fears.

Holding onto negative memories or emotions does nothing to hurt those who hurt us but instead works against ourselves increasing our own frustration in life. When people have done us wrong, we need them to know they have done us an injustice, whether or not the other person is sorry for what they have done to us. We need to forgive them, not for their benefit so much as for ourselves. Letting go of the hurt and anger is very important. Often in difficult times we learn we are resilient and discover some of our own strengths.

If your perspective has always been one of the "glass half-empty," change it. Become a little more optimistic and see that the glass is half-full and ready for you to fill it. What we think and what we think we know is our perception of our own reality, and our reality makes us who we are. If we change the way we think, ultimately our reality will change even if it is only in how we live and react to it.

Knowing who we are, what we like, what makes us happy, and what we like in people will help us develop better relationships with others. When we develop relationships with people like ourselves or who share our interests, we can create support mechanisms for each other. Our circle of friends and family helps us in the event of difficulty and in times when we need to share our joy and happiness.

As we create the support structure of people in our lives, we also need to strengthen our relationships with family and friends. Understand that our time and energy are our investments towards enriching relationships. Whether those relationships are with family, friends, neighbors, colleagues, or strangers, each contact with another person gives us an opportunity to share happiness.

Being able to say that we are able to experience peace and joy in our lives every day is another way of saying that we are generally happy in the face of difficult and hard times. Something that can help us through each day, especially in very difficult times, is hope.

Hope

Hope is the expectation that something better is possible. You will hear the term when there are expectations and desires for a certain thing or passion that wants to be fulfilled. Parents hear it when their children say "hope" in place of "want" and vice-versa. "Daddy/Mommy. I hope I get that truck, I really want that truck."

Hope comes into play when people are trying to push back a fear and in doing so use their energies and resources to make a situation or occurrence happen. "I hope I get …" a certain toy, a good grade, a job, a house, a loan, a friend/partner/boyfriend/ girlfriend, a life. These sayings are to counter the fear that what they want may not be achievable. Hope fights the fear within and helps the person find the energy to move forward and accomplish their goals.

With hope, peace and joy are possible because the element of fear and the corresponding feelings are pushed off so that the person can be open to the experience. Hope creates a new sense of possibility for that which we yearn, whether that is a job, possessions, friendship, or love. In times of hardship and amongst the strain of what is going on around us, hope makes the improbable feel possible. Though hard times do make it more difficult to notice possibilities and to imagine a better situation, with hope it is possible. Times of hope allow for freedoms from times of oppression, if only for brief moments. It can be said that during the Great Depression, people would find moments away from the sad realities. Some accepted the situation as a short journey in time with hopes for the better tomorrow, which allowed them to be able to be open to humor, peace, and joy.

Faith and belief

To not mention faith is to ignore that which is found at the core of most of humanity. Faith and beliefs are often engrained into us as children and open for debate and question as we age and have more experiences. Often when people think of faith or beliefs, the thought is to group them with churches, temples, synagogues, mosques, and other houses or buildings of organized religion. We will not delve into these distinctions but into the particular fact that having a faith or belief system is instrumental in finding peace and joy for people all around the world. This faith may have been formed within an organized religion, learned by exploration and experience, or philosophized to a point of belief without objective factual information to back such beliefs. We will explore how such faiths and beliefs assist in creating a life of peace and joy.

Often faith and belief in a certain philosophy or in a deity that is greater than we are can help us deal with the unknown. Those things in life that seem to contradict our expectations or where we need to deal with the disappointments that we can't comprehend at the time, can be explained or put into a comfortable perspective with the faiths and beliefs that comfort us. We want to know that in the end it will all make sense because of an ethereal being or our relationship in the cosmos.

When we have a strong faith, we are more able to act and work with conviction based on these faiths and beliefs. We will hold tight to the thoughts and beliefs and often ignore those people or situations that are counter to our beliefs. Whether or not we want to recognize the fact, we will hold biases and prejudices against others often because of our thought, beliefs, or faith. We may even condemn the other for their ignorance or maybe because of our arrogance in the idea that not only do they not share the same belief but they cannot recognize the truths we have come to know. Whether or not we are able to prove the reasons for our belief or faith, our confidence in our faith makes it possible for us to act when others may hesitate. Occasionally reexamining what we believe and how it effects our actions is very healthy and may help us avoid behaving in ways that are contrary to peace and love.

Wars, bigotry, condemnation, and attacks on individuals, societies, and whole races have been justified in the name of faith or a code of beliefs. The same beliefs that can help us more readily experience peace and joy are the same set of faith and beliefs that can cause people to kill, exploit, condemn, and create century-long wars based on the disagreement or the feeling of superiority of one over the other. Some faiths and beliefs can be the cause for our own condemnation, dysfunction, and isolation. Ultimately it is up to the individual to decide whether or not their actions on any given day are guided by their faith or belief. When we live the life we believe to be correct, we can experience peace in the knowledge that our actions and lives are right and our conscience is clear. It is our faith and belief that defines what we know to be correct. Our conscience is what we have made it to be, and it is what will determine whether we can accept peace and joy in our lives.

Questioning our beliefs is not the point, but rather questioning how we have acted on these beliefs and what that has brought us. If our lives don't emulate the ideals we value or if that faith is more constraining than freeing, then it is time to reassess our belief systems. As children we are told to listen, learn, and believe. As adults we are to listen, learn, analyze, and ponder what we know, what we believe, and how we live our lives. Faith and belief is often a vital part to the process toward a life of peace and joy.

Love

The ultimate outcome to peace and joy is love. When we are generally happy, we are able to think more of others than ourselves. Peace and joy gives us the chance to become stronger individuals with the endurance, fortitude, and compassion for ourselves and others. Our relationships grow, and our ability to feel empathy for others will enrich our relationships and the love we have for people in general. To put ourselves in "other people's shoes" will expand our understanding of others and the ability to forgive wrongs that happen to us. True peace and joy in life also gives us the opportunity to find happiness in everything and see the possibilities of life we were not able to see before. To live a life of peace is to love more greatly.

Often when we are in the midst of despair or are suffering injustice, it becomes ever so difficult to think of others. When life is going smoothly or we feel like we are doing well, our ability to see the plights of others becomes easier. During holidays, many non-profit organizations have a sudden increase in donations and assistance by first time or annual donors. This is in part due to the increased feeling of happiness and charity. This charity is a form of love of our neighbor. By caring for a person we may never know or meet, we cherish the knowledge that another human being is going to have a better day because of the generosity we share. On the other hand, when a person is undergoing grief or hardship without the assistance of hope and the support of others, being generous and sharing happiness seems distant or unthink-able. Some may even despise those cheerful people around them and become the Scrooges in such celebrations. Those of us who are able to experience peace and joy can share happiness with others by actions of kindness and charity. This is often the hope and shared happiness that can help others in the midst despair. Whether we want to acknowledge it or not, charity is the sign of love for the stranger, not for any particular reason other than their humanity.

Having experienced peace and joy in our individual lives, we are able to be steadfast for those whom we care for and love. Parents who work tirelessly to give their children and family a chance at a better life even in times of financial hardship and personal sacrifice endure the difficult times and are driven by love. The single parent tries to be both mother and father to their children, while working and being an active homemaker, even though fatigue and worry confront the individual daily. A neighbor helping the elderly person next door by cutting their grass without the thanks or acknowledgement of such kindness is able to endure because they do not need the recognition. Happiness in one's personal life and peace in a person's heart brings a joy in actions that ripple to those around them. This is when peace and joy is shared and can carry a person who otherwise would be stretched too thin to care.

Love is the manifestation of peace and joy in our lives, which expands in our understanding of ourselves and drives us to look for the good in others. People living in peace and general happiness have no use, need, or want for any mask or façade. Humility in knowing the negative and positive traits and characteristics of ourselves and coming to terms with our personal insecurities gives us a great sense of peace. This also provides us a way to be able to see the best in others, the potential in the stranger, and the happiness that can be shared. It is harder to fear rejection if we can accept others for who they are. In so doing we build compassion, empathy, and a greater understanding of the human condition.

Famous people such as Mahatma Gandhi, Mother Teresa of Calcutta, Martin Luther King Jr., and other well-known activists for peace and understanding often spoke of love—love for our families, friends, neighbors, strangers, and even enemies. These same people had come to terms with their own insecurities, challenges, positive traits, and the limitations in society, and yet they are memorialized for their teaching of compassion, understanding, forgiveness, patience, and unconditional love.

Living in a state of happiness every day is not to dismiss the fact that we may have to deal with real problems and challenges that life may throw at us. There will be times of sadness and anxiety and a hope those times will improve. What makes it ultimately possible to live a life that is generally happy and based on peace and joy stems from our perspective, the relationships we have with those around us, and our ability to be at peace with ourselves. When we can see the good in our lives even amidst difficult times, we can remain generally happy and often can be a catalyst for peace and joy for others. This will only help our relationships grow and enrich our lives. Ultimately the peace and joy we have will spill out to those around us in the form of kindness, understanding, charity, and a love free from conditions, exclusions, or perversions. It is in the search of joy and the living in peace that we can exist happily even in the midst of challenges we experience every day.

About the Author

After receiving much encouragement and excitement from those she had helped over the years, Yvonne B. Gray started to put her observations and advice onto the printed page. Her dedication to teaching and helping others is evident in her education and experience starting off in the scientific community and bridging over to teaching individuals and groups in collegiate and private forums. Having grown up in a military family at home and abroad, Gray appreciates and recognizes many experiences from various walks of life. Her innate understanding of family dynamics stems from her education and personal experience of raising six children while completing multiple college degrees. Gray currently resides in Colorado and continues to help numerous individuals maneuver everyday challenges.

www.FindingPeaceDiscoveringJoy.com

www.YBGray.com